the
cult of the
amateur

the
cult of the
amateur

how today's internet is
killing our culture

andrew keen

Doubleday / Currency
New York London Toronto Sydney Auckland

A CURRENCY BOOK
PUBLISHED BY DOUBLEDAY

Copyright © 2007 by Andrew Keen

Book design by Chris Welch

Library of Congress Cataloging-in-Publication Data
Keen, Andrew.
The cult of the amateur : how today's internet is killing our culture /
Andrew Keen. — 1st ed.
p. cm.
1. Internet—Social aspects. 2. Internet—Economic aspects. 3. Social
change. 4. Information society. 5. Self-publishing. I. Title.

HM851.K44 2007
303.48'33—dc22

2006103058

ISBN 978-0-385-52080-5

PRINTED IN THE UNITED STATES OF AMERICA

1 3 5 7 9 10 8 6 4 2

First Edition

For Elias, Zara, and Betsy.

contents

the
cult of the
amateur

introduction

f I didn't know better, I'd think it was 1999 all over again. The boom has returned to Silicon Valley, and the mad utopians are once again running wild. I bumped into one such evangelist at a recent San Francisco mixer.

Over glasses of fruity local Chardonnay, we swapped notes about our newest new things. He told me his current gig involved a new software for publishing music, text, and video on the Internet.

"It's MySpace meets YouTube meets Wikipedia meets Google," he said. "On steroids."

In reply, I explained I was working on a polemic about the destructive impact of the digital revolution on our culture, economy, and values.

"It's ignorance meets egoism meets bad taste meets mob rule," I said, unable to resist a smile. "On steroids."

He smiled uneasily in return. "So it's Huxley meets the digital age," he said. "You're rewriting Huxley for the twenty-first century." He raised his wine glass in my honor. "To *Brave New World 2.0!*"

We clinked wine glasses. But I knew we were toasting the wrong Huxley. Rather than Aldous, the inspiration behind this book comes from his grandfather, T. H. Huxley, the nineteenth-century evolutionary biologist and author of the "infinite monkey theorem." Huxley's theory says that if you provide infinite monkeys with infinite typewriters, some monkey somewhere will eventually create a masterpiece—a play by Shakespeare, a Platonic dialogue, or an economic treatise by Adam Smith.[1]

In the pre-Internet age, T. H. Huxley's scenario of infinite monkeys empowered with infinite technology seemed more like a mathematical jest than a dystopian vision. But what had once appeared as a joke now seems to foretell the consequences of a flattening of culture that is blurring the lines between traditional audience and author, creator and consumer, expert and amateur. This is no laughing matter.

Today's technology hooks all those monkeys up with all those typewriters. Except in our Web 2.0 world, the typewriters aren't quite typewriters, but rather networked personal computers, and the monkeys aren't quite monkeys, but rather Internet users. And instead of creating masterpieces, these millions and millions of exuberant monkeys—many with no more talent in the creative arts than our primate cousins—are creating an endless digital forest of mediocrity. For today's amateur monkeys can use their networked computers to publish everything from uninformed political commentary, to unseemly home videos, to embarrassingly amateurish music, to unreadable poems, reviews, essays, and novels.

At the heart of this infinite monkey experiment in self-publishing is the Internet diary, the ubiquitous blog. Blogging has become such a mania that a new blog is being created every second of every minute of every hour of every day. We are blogging with monkeylike shamelessness about our private lives, our sex lives, our dream lives, our lack of lives, our Second Lives. At the time of writing there are fifty-three million blogs on the Internet, and this number is doubling every six months. In the time it took you to read this paragraph, ten new blogs were launched.

If we keep up this pace, there will be over five hundred million blogs by 2010, collectively corrupting and confusing popular opinion about everything from politics, to commerce, to arts and culture. Blogs have become so dizzyingly infinite that they've undermined our sense of what is true and what is false, what is real and what is imaginary. These days, kids can't tell the difference between credible news by objective professional journalists and what they read on joeshmoe.blogspot.com. For these Generation Y utopians, every posting is just another person's version of the truth; every fiction is just another person's version of the facts.

Then there is Wikipedia, an online encyclopedia where anyone with opposable thumbs and a fifth-grade education can publish anything on any topic from AC/DC to Zoroastrianism. Since Wikipedia's birth, more than fifteen thousand contributors have created nearly three million entries in over a hundred different languages—none of them edited or vetted for accuracy. With hundreds of thousands of visitors a day, Wikipedia has become the third most visited site for information and current events; a more trusted source for news than the CNN or BBC Web sites, even though Wikipedia has no reporters, no editorial staff, and no experience in newsgathering. It's the blind leading the blind—infinite monkeys providing infinite information for infinite readers, perpetuating the cycle of misinformation and ignorance.

On Wikipedia, everyone with an agenda can rewrite an entry to their liking—and contributors frequently do. *Forbes* recently reported, for example, a story of anonymous McDonald and Wal-Mart employees furtively using Wikipedia entries as a medium for deceptively spreading corporate propaganda. On the McDonald's entry, a link to Eric Schlosser's *Fast Food Nation* conveniently disappeared; on Wal-Mart's somebody eliminated a line about underpaid employees making less than 20 percent of the competition.[2]

But the Internet's infinite monkey experiment is not limited to the written word. T. H. Huxley's nineteenth-century typewriter has evolved into not only the computer, but also the camcorder, turning the Internet into a vast library for user-generated video content. One site, YouTube, is a portal of amateur videos that, at the time of writing, was the world's fastest-growing site,[3] attracting sixty-five thousand new videos daily and boasting sixty million clips being watched each day; that adds up to over twenty-five million new videos a year,[4] and some twenty-five billion hits. In the fall of 2006, this overnight sensation was bought by Google for over a billion and a half dollars.

YouTube eclipses even the blogs in the inanity and absurdity of its content. Nothing seems too prosaic or narcissistic for these videographer monkeys. The site is an infinite gallery of amateur movies showing poor fools dancing, singing, eating, washing, shopping, driving, cleaning, sleeping, or just staring into their computers. In August 2006, one hugely popular video called "The Easter Bunny Hates You" showed a man in a bunny suit harassing and attacking people on the streets; according to *Forbes* magazine, this video was viewed more than three million times in two weeks. A few other favorite subjects include a young woman watching another YouTube user who is watching yet another user—a virtual hall of mirrors that eventually leads to a woman making a peanut butter and jelly sandwich in front of the television; a Malaysian dancer in absurdly short skirts grooving to Ricky Martin and Britney Spears; a dog chasing its tail; an Englishwoman instructing her viewers how to eat a chocolate and marmalade cookie; and, in a highly appropriate addition to the YouTube library, a video of dancing stuffed monkeys.

What's more disturbing than the fact that millions of us willingly tune in to such nonsense each day is that some Web sites are making monkeys out of us without our even knowing it. By entering words into Google's search engine, we are actually creating something called "collective intelligence," the sum wisdom of all Google users. The logic of Google's search engine, what technologists call its algorithm, reflects the "wisdom" of the crowd. In other words, the more people click on a link that results from a search, the more likely that link will come up in subsequent searches. The search engine is an aggregation of the ninety million questions we collectively ask Google each day; in other words, it just tells us what we already know.

This same "wisdom" of the crowd is manifested on editor-free news-aggregation sites such as Digg and Reddit. The ordering of the headlines on these sites reflects what other users have been reading rather than the expert judgment of news editors. As I write, there is a brutal war going on in Lebanon between Israel and Hezbollah. But the Reddit user wouldn't know this because there is nothing about Israel, Lebanon, or Hezbollah on the site's top twenty "hot" stories. Instead, subscribers can read about a flat-chested English actress, the walking habits of elephants, a spoof of the latest Mac commercial, and underground tunnels in Japan. Reddit is a mirror of our most banal interests. It makes a mockery of traditional news media and turns current events into a childish game of Trivial Pursuit.

The *New York Times* reports that 50 percent of all bloggers blog for the sole purpose of reporting and sharing experiences about their personal lives. The tagline for YouTube is "Broadcast Yourself." And broadcast ourselves we do, with all the shameless self-admiration of the mythical Narcissus. As traditional mainstream media is replaced by a personalized one, the Internet has become a mirror to ourselves. Rather than using it to seek news, information, or culture, we use it to actually BE the news, the information, the culture.

This infinite desire for personal attention is driving the hottest part of the new Internet economy—social-networking sites like MySpace, Facebook, and Bebo. As shrines for the cult of self-broadcasting, these sites have become tabula rasas of our individual desires and identities. They claim to be all about "social networking" with others, but in reality they exist so that we can advertise ourselves: everything from our favorite books and movies, to photos from our summer vacations, to "testimonials" praising our more winsome qualities or recapping our latest drunken exploits. It's hardly surprising that the increasingly tasteless nature of such self-advertisements has led to an infestation of anonymous sexual predators and pedophiles.

But our cultural standards and moral values are not all that are at stake. Gravest of all, the very traditional institutions that have helped to foster and create our news, our music, our literature, our television shows, and our movies are under assault as well. Newspapers and newsmagazines, one of the most reliable sources of information about the world we live in, are flailing, thanks to the proliferation of free blogs and sites like Craigslist that offer free classifieds, undermining paid ad placements. In the first quarter of 2006, profits plummeted dramatically at all the major newspaper companies—down 69 percent at the New York Times Company, 28 percent at the Tribune Company, and 11 percent at Gannett, the nation's largest newspaper company. Circulation is down, too. At the *San Francisco Chronicle,* ironically one of the newspapers of record for Silicon Valley, readership was down a dizzying 16 percent in the middle two quarters of 2005 alone.[5] And in 2007, Time, Inc., laid off almost 300 people, primarily from editorial, from such magazines as *Time, People,* and *Sports Illustrated.*

Those of us who still read the newspaper and magazines know that people are buying less music, too. Thanks to the rampant digital piracy spawned by file-sharing technology, sales of recorded music dropped over 20 percent between 2000 and 2006.[6]

In parallel with the rise of YouTube, Hollywood is experiencing its own financial troubles. Domestic box office sales now represent less than 20 percent of Hollywood's revenue and, with the levelling off of DVD sales and the rampant global piracy, the industry is desperately searching for a new business model that will enable it to profitably distribute movies on the Internet. According to *The New Yorker* film critic David Denby, many studio executives in Hollywood are now in a "panic" over declining revenue. One bleak consequence is cuts. Disney, for example, announced 650 job cuts in 2006, and an almost 50 percent drop in the number of animated movies produced annually.[7]

Old media is facing extinction. But if so, what will take its place? Apparently, it will be Silicon Valley's hot new search engines, social media sites, and video portals. Every new page on MySpace, every new blog post, every new YouTube video adds up to another potential source of advertising revenue lost to mainstream media. Thus, Rupert Murdoch's canny—or desperate—decision in July 2005 to buy MySpace for five hundred and eighty million dollars. Thus, the $1.65 billion sale of YouTube and the explosion of venture capital funding YouTube copycat sites. And, thus, the seemingly unstoppable growth at Google where, in the second quarter of 2006, revenue surged to almost two and a half billion dollars.

What happens, you might ask, when ignorance meets egoism meets bad taste meets mob rule?

The monkeys take over. Say good-bye to today's experts and cultural gatekeepers—our reporters, news anchors, editors, music companies, and Hollywood movie studios. In today's cult of the amateur,[8] the monkeys are running the show. With their infinite typewriters, they are authoring the future. And we may not like how it reads.

1

the great seduction

First a confession. Back in the Nineties, I was a pioneer in the first Internet gold rush. With the dream of making the world a more musical place, I founded Audiocafe.com, one of the earliest digital music sites. Once, when asked by a San Francisco Bay area newspaper reporter how I wanted to change the world, I replied, half seriously, that my fantasy was to have music playing from "every orifice," to hear the whole Bob Dylan oeuvre from my laptop computer, to be able to download Johann Sebastian Bach's Brandenburg Concertos from my cellular phone.

So yes, I peddled the original Internet dream. I seduced investors and I almost became rich. This, therefore, is no ordinary critique of Silicon Valley. It's the work of an apostate, an insider now on the outside who has poured out his cup of Kool-Aid and resigned his membership in the cult.

My metamorphosis from believer into skeptic lacks cinematic drama. I didn't break down while reading an incorrect Wikipedia entry about T. H. Huxley or get struck by lightning while doing a search for myself on Google. My epiphany didn't involve a dancing coyote, so it probably wouldn't be a hit on YouTube.

It took place over forty-eight hours, in September 2004, on a two-day camping trip with a couple of hundred Silicon Valley utopians. Sleeping bag under my arm, rucksack on my back, I marched into camp a member of the cult; two days later, feeling queasy, I left an unbeliever.

The camping trip took place in Sebastopol, a small farming town in northern California's Sonoma Valley, about fifty miles north of the infamous Silicon Valley—the narrow peninsula of land between San Francisco and San Jose. Sebastopol is the headquarters of O'Reilly Media, one of the world's leading traffickers of books, magazines, and trade shows about information technology, an evangelizer of innovation to a worldwide congregation of technophiles. It is both Silicon Valley's most fervent preacher and its noisiest chorus.

Each Fall, O'Reilly Media hosts an exclusive, invitation-only event called FOO (Friends of O'Reilly) Camp. These friends of multi-millionaire founder Tim O'Reilly are not only unconventionally rich and richly unconventional but also harbor a messianic faith in the economic and cultural benefits of technology. O'Reilly and his Silicon Valley acolytes are a mix of graying hippies, new media entreprencurs, and technology geeks. What unites them is a shared hostility toward traditional media and entertainment. Part Woodstock, part Burning Man (the contemporary festival of self-expression held in a desert in Nevada), and part Stanford Business School retreat, FOO Camp is where the countercultural Sixties meets the free-market Eighties meets the technophile Nineties.

Silicon Valley conferences weren't new to me. I had even organized one myself at the tail end of the last Internet boom. But FOO Camp was radically different. Its only rule was an unrule: "no spectators, only participants." The camp was run on open-source, Wikipedia-style participatory principles—which meant that everyone talked a lot, and there was no one in charge.

So there we were, two hundred of us, Silicon Valley's antiestablishment establishment, collectively worth hundreds of millions of dollars, gazing at the stars from the lawn of O'Reilly Media's corporate headquarters. For two full days, we camped together, roasted marshmallows together, and celebrated the revival of our cult together.

The Internet was back! And unlike the Gold Rush Nineties, this time around our exuberance wasn't irrational. This shiny new version of the Internet, what Tim O'Reilly called Web 2.0, really was going to change everything. Now that most Americans had broadband access to the Internet, the dream of a fully networked, always-connected society was finally going to be realized.

There was one word on every FOO Camper's lips in September 2004. That word was "democratization."

I never realized democracy has so many possibilities, so much revolutionary potential. Media, information, knowledge, content, audience, author—all were going to be *democratized* by Web 2.0. The Internet would *democratize* Big Media, Big Business, Big Government. It would even *democratize* Big Experts, transforming them into what one friend of O'Reilly called, in a hushed, reverent tone, "noble amateurs."

Although Sebastopol was miles from the ocean, by the second morning of camp, I had begun to feel seasick. At first I thought it was the greasy camp food or perhaps the hot northern California weather. But I soon realized that even my gut was reacting to the emptiness at the heart of our conversation.

I had come to FOO Camp to imagine the future of media. I wanted to know how the Internet could help me "bring more music to more orifices." But my dream of making the world a more musical place had fallen on deaf ears; the promise of using technology to bring *more* culture to the masses had been drowned out by FOO Campers' collective cry for a democratized media.

The new Internet was about self-made music, not Bob Dylan or the Brandenburg Concertos. Audience and author had become one, and we were transforming culture into cacophony.

FOO Camp, I realized, was a sneak preview. We weren't there just to talk about new media; we *were* the new media. The event was a beta version of the Web 2.0 revolution, where Wikipedia met MySpace met YouTube. Everyone was simultaneously broadcasting themselves, but nobody was listening. Out of this anarchy, it suddenly became clear that what was governing the infinite monkeys now inputting away on the Internet was the law of digital Darwinism, the survival of the loudest and most opinionated. Under these rules, the only way to intellectually prevail is by infinite filibustering.

The more that was said that weekend, the less I wanted to express myself. As the din of narcissism swelled, I became increasingly silent. And thus began my rebellion against Silicon Valley. Instead of adding to the noise, I broke the one law of FOO Camp 2004. I stopped participating and sat back and watched.

I haven't stopped watching since. I've spent the last two years observing the Web 2.0 revolution, and I'm dismayed by what I've seen.

I've seen the infinite monkeys, of course, typing away. And I've seen many other strange sights as well, including a video of marching penguins selling a lie, a supposedly infinite Long Tail, and dogs chatting to each other online. But what I've been watching is more like Hitchcock's *The Birds* than *Doctor Doolittle:* a horror movie about the consequences of the digital revolution.

Because democratization, despite its lofty idealization, is undermining truth, souring civic discourse, and belittling expertise, experience, and talent. As I noted earlier, it is threatening the very future of our cultural institutions.

I call it the great seduction. The Web 2.0 revolution has peddled the promise of bringing more truth to more people—more depth of information, more global perspective, more unbiased opinion from dispassionate observers. But this is all a smokescreen. What the Web 2.0 revolution is really delivering is superficial observations of the world around us rather than deep analysis, shrill opinion rather than considered judgment. The information business is being transformed by the Internet into the sheer noise of a hundred million bloggers all simultaneously talking about themselves.

Moreover, the free, user-generated content spawned and extolled by the Web 2.0 revolution is decimating the ranks of our cultural gatekeepers, as professional critics, journalists, editors, musicians, moviemakers, and other purveyors of expert information are being replaced ("disintermediated," to use a FOO Camp term) by amateur bloggers, hack reviewers, homespun moviemakers, and attic recording artists. Meanwhile, the radically new business models based on user-generated material suck the economic value out of traditional media and cultural content.

We—those of us who want to know more about the world, those of us who are the consumers of mainstream culture—are being seduced by the empty promise of the "democratized" media. For the real consequence of the Web 2.0 revolution is less culture, less reliable news, and a chaos of useless information. One chilling reality in this brave new digital epoch is the blurring, obfuscation, and even disappearance of truth.

Truth, to paraphrase Tom Friedman, is being "flattened," as we create an on-demand, personalized version that reflects our own individual myopia. One person's truth becomes as "true" as anyone else's. Today's media is shattering the world into a billion personalized truths, each seemingly equally valid and worthwhile. To quote Richard Edelman, the founder, president, and CEO of Edelman PR, the world's largest privately owned public relations company:

> In this era of exploding media technologies there is no truth except the truth you create for yourself.[1]

This undermining of truth is threatening the quality of civil public discourse, encouraging plagiarism and intellectual property theft, and stifling creativity. When advertising and public relations are disguised as news, the line between fact and fiction becomes blurred. Instead of more community, knowledge, or culture, all that Web 2.0 really delivers is more dubious content from anonymous sources, hijacking our time and playing to our gullibility.

Need proof? Let's look at that army of perjurious penguins—"Al Gore's Army of Penguins" to be exact. Featured on YouTube, the film, a crude "self-made" satire of Gore's pro-environment movie *An Inconvenient Truth,* belittles the seriousness of Al Gore's message by depicting a penguin version of Al Gore preaching to other penguins about global warning.

But "Al Gore's Army of Penguins" is not just another homemade example of YouTube inanity. Though many of the 120,000 people who viewed this video undoubtedly assumed it was the work of some SUV-driving amateur with an aversion to recycling, in reality, the *Wall Street Journal* traced the real authorship of this neocon satire to DCI Group, a conservative Washington, D.C., public relationships and lobbying firm whose clients include Exxon-Mobil.[2] The video is nothing more than political spin, enabled and perpetuated by the anonymity of Web 2.0, masquerading as independent art. In short, it is a big lie.

Blogs too, can be vehicles for veiled corporate propaganda and deception. In March 2006, the *New York Times* reported about a blogger whose laudatory postings about Wal-Mart were "identical" to press releases written by a senior account supervisor at the Arkansas retailer's PR company.[3] Perhaps this is the same team behind the mysterious elimination of unflattering remarks about Wal-Mart's treatment of its employees on the retailer's Wikipedia entry.

Blogs are increasingly becoming the battlefield on which public relations spin doctors are waging their propaganda war. In 2005, before launching a major investment, General Electric executives met with environmental bloggers to woo them over the greenness of a new energy-efficient technology. Meanwhile, multinationals like IBM, Maytag, and General Motors all have blogs that, under an objective guise, peddle their versions of corporate truth to the outside world.

But the anticorporate blogs are equally loose with the truth. In 2005, when the famous and fictitious finger-in-the-chili story broke, every anti-Wendy's blogger jumped on it as evidence of fast-food malfeasance. The bogus story cost Wendy's $2.5 million in lost sales as well as job losses and a decline in the price of the company's stock.

As former British Prime Minister James Callaghan said, "A lie can make its way around the world before the truth has the chance to put its boots on." That has never been more true than with the speeding, freewheeling, unchecked culture of today's blogosphere.

It doesn't require the gravitas of a world leader to appreciate the implications of this democratized media. In a flattened, editor-free world where independent videographers, podcasters, and bloggers can post their amateurish creations at will, and no one is being paid to check their credentials or evaluate their material, media is vulnerable to untrustworthy content of every stripe—whether from duplicitous PR companies, multinational corporations like Wal-Mart and McDonald's, anonymous bloggers, or sexual predators with sophisticated invented identities.

Who is to say, for example, that a Malaysian prostitution ring didn't sponsor the famous YouTube video of the sexy Malaysian dancer? Or that the Englishwoman in the YouTube video eating the chocolate and marmalade cookie isn't really being paid by United Biscuits Incorporated?

Who is to say that the glowing review of *The Cult of the Amateur* on Amazon.com that might have led you to purchase this "brilliantly original" book wasn't authored by me, posing as an enthusiastic third party?

As I'll discuss in more detail in Chapter 3, truth and trust are the whipping boys of the Web 2.0 revolution. In a world with fewer and fewer professional editors or reviewers, how are we to know what and whom to believe? Because much of the user-generated content on the Internet is posted anonymously or under a pseudonym, nobody knows who the real author of much of this self-generated content actually is. It could be a monkey. It could be a penguin. It could even be Al Gore.

Look at Wikipedia, the Internet's largest cathedral of knowledge. Unlike editors at a professional encyclopedia like the *Britannica*, the identity of the volunteer editors on Wikipedia is unknown. These citizen editors out-edit other citizen editors in defining, redefining, then rere-defining truth, sometimes hundreds of times a day. Take, for example, July 5, 2006, the day Enron embezzler Ken Lay died. At 10:06 A.M. that day, the Wikipedia entry about Lay said he died of an "apparent suicide." Two minutes later, it said that the cause of death was an "apparent heart attack." Then at 10:11 A.M., Wikipedia reported that the "guilt of ruining so many lives finally led him to his suicide."[4] At 10:12, we were back to the massive coronary causing Lay's demise. And in February 2007, just minutes after ex-*Playboy* Playmate Anna Nicole Smith died in Florida, her Wikipedia page was flooded with conflicting, speculative versions of the cause of death. As Marshall Poe observed in the September 2006 issue of the *Atlantic:*

> We tend to think of truth as something that resides in the world. The fact that two plus two equals four is written in the stars. . . . But Wikipedia suggests a different *theory of truth*. Just think about the way we learn what words mean. . . . The community decides that two plus two equals four the same way it decides what an apple is: by consensus. Yes, that means that if the community changes its mind and decides that two plus two equals five, then *two plus two does equal five*. The community isn't likely to do such an absurd or useless thing, but it has the ability.[5]

In Orwell's *Nineteen Eighty-Four,* Big Brother insisted that two plus two equaled five, transforming a patently incorrect statement into the state-sanctioned, official truth. Today, as I discuss in Chapter 7, there is potentially an even more threatening Big Brother lurking in the shadows: the search engine. We pour our innermost secrets into the all-powerful search engine through the tens of millions of questions we enter daily. Search engines like Google know more about our habits, our interests, our desires than our friends, our loved ones, and our shrink combined. But unlike in *Nineteen Eighty-Four,* this Big Brother is very much for real. We have to trust it not to spill our secrets—a trust, as we will see, that has repeatedly been betrayed.

Paradoxically enough, the holy grail of advertisers in the flattened world of the Web 2.0 is to achieve the trust of others. And it is turning the conventional advertising industry upside down. MySpace, according to the *Wall Street Journal* and other papers, now runs profiles of fictional characters in an attempt to market certain products by creating "personal relationships with millions of young people." News Corp. (which owns MySpace) has bought the right to include profiles of fictional characters such as Ricky Bobby (played by Will Ferrell) from the 2006 blockbuster *Talladega Nights.* Other recent members of the MySpace community include advertising vehicles like Gil, the crab from the Honda Element commercials; Burger King's royal mascot; and a character called "Miss Irresistible," the gleaming-toothed spokesperson for a new version of Crest toothpaste. But are Gil, the Burger King king, and Miss Irresistible really our friends? No. They are fictional characters whose only purpose is to sell our impressionable kids more toothpaste and hamburgers.

Our trust in conventional advertising is being further compromised by the spoof advertisements proliferating on the Internet. For example, the *New York Times* reported on August 15, 2006, that at the time, over 100 videos mocking an ad campaign launched by the Internet phone provider Vonage were posted on YouTube, and that many had been viewed at least 5,000 times. These amateurish, unauthorized send-ups of popular commercials are rarely flattering, and typically invent or expose flaws in a brand or a product. However, to the chagrin of ad executives (the interactive creative director for Crispin, Porter & Bogusky likens the phenomenon to "brand terrorism on the internet"), the homemade videos are often cobbled together from clips of actual advertisements, making the knockoffs often indistinguishable from the real commercials.

Our attitudes about "authorship," too, are undergoing a radical change as a result of today's democratized Internet culture. In a world in which audience and author are increasingly indistinguishable, and where authenticity is almost impossible to verify, the idea of original authorship and intellectual property has been seriously compromised. Who "owns" the content created by the fictional movie characters on MySpace? Who "owns" the content created by an anonymous hive of Wikipedia editors? Who "owns" the content posted by bloggers, whether it originates from corporate spin doctors or from articles in the *New York Times*? This nebulous definition of ownership, compounded by the ease in which we can now cut and paste other people's work to make it appear as if it's ours, has resulted in a troubling new permissiveness about intellectual property.

Cutting and pasting, of course, is child's play on the Web 2.0, enabling a younger generation of intellectual kleptomaniacs, who think their ability to cut and paste a well-phrased thought or opinion makes it their own. Original file-sharing technologies like Napster and Kazaa, which gained so much attention during the first Web boom, pale in comparison to the latest Web 2.0 "remixing" of content and "mashing up" of software and music. In a twisted kind of Alice in Wonderland, down-the-rabbit-hole logic, Silicon Valley visionaries such as Stanford law professor and Creative Commons founder Lawrence Lessig and cyberpunk author William Gibson laud the appropriation of intellectual property. As Gibson wrote in the July 2005 issue of *Wired* magazine:

> Our culture no longer bothers to use words like *appropriation* or *borrowing* to describe those very activities. Today's audience isn't listening at all—it's participating. Indeed, *audience* is as antique a term as *record*, the one archaically passive, the other archaically physical. The record, not the remix, is the anomaly today. The remix is the very nature of the digital.

Top students at Britain's Oxford University are heeding Gibson's advice; in June 2006, the *Guardian* newspaper reported that the university's reputation was "under threat as students increasingly copied slabs of work from the Internet and submitted it as their own." A survey published in *Education Week* found that 54 percent of students admitted to plagiarizing from the Internet. And who is to know if the other 46 percent are telling the truth? Copyright and authorship begin to lose all meaning to those posting their mash-ups and remixings on the

Web. They are, as Professor Sally Brown at Leeds Metropolitan University notes, "Postmodern, eclectic, Google-generationists, Wikipediasts, who don't necessarily recognize the concepts of authorships/ownerships."

The intellectual consequences of such theft are profoundly disturbing. Gibson's culture of the ubiquitous remix is not only destroying the sanctity of authorship but also undermining our traditional safeguards of individual creativity. The value once placed on a book by a great author is being challenged by the dream of a collective hyperlinked community of authors who endlessly annotate and revise it, forever conversing with each other in a never-ending loop of self-references.

Kevin Kelly, in a May 2006 *New York Times Magazine* article,[6] rhapsodizes over the death of the traditional stand-alone text—what centuries of civilization have known as the book. What Kelly envisions instead is an infinitely interconnected media in which all the world's books are digitally scanned and linked together: what he calls the "liquid version" of the book. In Kelly's view, the act of cutting and pasting and linking and annotating a text is as or more important than the writing of the book in the first place. It is the literary version of Wikipedia. Instead of traditional books by the Norman Mailers, Alice Walkers, and John Updikes, we should embrace, according to Kelly, a single, hyperlinked, communal, digital text that is edited and annotated by amateurs.

So what happens when you combine Kelly's liquid version of the book with a wiki? You get a million penguins.

That's actually the title of De Montford University's January 2007 "wiki-novel,"[7] a democratic literary experiment sponsored by the British publisher Penguin, which invites anyone to contribute to a collective online novel. But can a collaboration of amateur voices create an authoritative, coherent fictional narrative? I doubt it. As Penguin blogger and literary critic Jon Elek wrote, "I'll be happy so long as it manages to avoid becoming some sort of robotic-zombie-assassins-against-African-ninjas-in-space-narrated-by-a-Papal-Tiara type of thing."[8]

It is not just our aesthetic sensibilities that are under assault. The Internet has become the medium of choice for distorting the truth about politics and politicians on both sides of the fence. The 2004 attack on John Kerry's Swift Boat record in Vietnam, for example, was orchestrated by hundreds of conservative bloggers who painted a patriotic American public servant as a patsy for Vietcong propaganda. And what about the left-wing blogosphere's assault, in the summer and fall of 2006, on Joe Lieberman, the centrist Democratic Connecticut senator, who attackers dressed up as a right-wing, Bush-loving, warmongering Republican, costing him the 2006 primary (he, of course, went on to win the general election, vindicating himself in the end). None of these blogs, from MoveOn.org to Swiftvets.com, seriously debate the issues or address the ambiguities and complexity of politics. Instead, they cater to an increasingly partisan minority that uses "democratized" digital media to obfuscate truth and manipulate public opinion.

The Cost of Democratization

This blurring of lines between the audience and the author, between fact and fiction, between invention and reality further obscures objectivity. The cult of the amateur has made it increasingly difficult to determine the difference between reader and writer, between artist and spin doctor, between art and advertisement, between amateur and expert. The result? The decline of the quality and reliability of the information we receive, thereby distorting, if not outrightly corrupting, our national civic conversation.

But perhaps the biggest casualties of the Web 2.0 revolution are real businesses with real products, real employees, and real shareholders, as I'll discuss in Chapters 4 and 5. Every defunct record label, or laid-off newspaper reporter, or bankrupt independent bookstore is a consequence of "free" user-generated Internet content—from Craigslist's free advertising, to YouTube's free music videos, to Wikipedia's free information.

What you may not realize is that what is free is actually costing us a fortune. The new winners—Google, YouTube, MySpace, Craigslist, and the hundreds of start-ups all hungry for a piece of the Web 2.0 pie—are unlikely to fill the shoes of the industries they are helping to undermine, in terms of products produced, jobs created, revenue generated, or benefits conferred. By stealing away our eyeballs, the blogs and wikis are decimating the publishing, music, and news-gathering industries that created the original content those Web sites "aggregate." Our culture is essentially cannibalizing its young, destroying the very sources of the content they crave. Can that be the new business model of the twenty-first century?

A *Business 2.0* July 2006 cover story asked who are the fifty people "who matter most" in the new economy. Leading the list was not Steve Jobs or Rupert Murdoch or Sergey Brin and Larry Page, the two founders of Google. It was "YOU! The Consumer as Creator":

> You—or rather, the collaborative intelligence of tens of millions of people, the networked you— continually create and filter new forms of content, anointing the useful, the relevant, and the amusing and rejecting the rest. . . . In every case, you've become an integral part of the action as a member of the aggregated, interactive, self-organizing, auto-entertaining audience.

Who was *Time* magazine's 2006 Person of the Year? Was it George W. Bush, or Pope Benedict XVI, or Bill Gates and Warren Buffett, who together contributed more than $70 billion of their wealth to improving life on earth? None of the above. *Time* gave the award to YOU:

> Yes, you. You control the Information Age. Welcome to your world.

This same YOU! rules Wikipedia, where the knowledge consumer is also the knowledge creator. YOU! defines YouTube, where the tens of thousands of daily videos are both produced and watched by one and the same. YOU! are both ordering and reviewing books on Amazon.com, bidding and auctioning goods on eBay, buying and designing video games on Microsoft's Xbox platform, and listing and responding to advertisements on Craigslist.

Of course, every free listing on Craigslist means one less paid listing in a local newspaper. Every visit to Wikipedia's free information hive means one less customer for a professionally researched and edited encyclopedia such as *Britannica*. Every free music or video upload is one less sale of a CD or DVD, meaning one less royalty for the artist who created it.

In his recent bestselling book *The Long Tail*,[9] *Wired* magazine editor Chris Anderson celebrates this flattening of culture, which he describes as the end of the hit parade. In Anderson's brave new world, there will be infinite shelf space for infinite products, thus giving everyone infinite choice. *The Long Tail* virtually redefines the word "economics"—shifting it from the science of scarcity to the science of abundancy, and promising an infinite market in which we cycle and recycle our cultural production to our hearts' content. It's a seductive notion. But even if one accepts Anderson's dubious economic arguments, the Long Tail theory has a glaring hole. Anderson assumes that raw talent is as infinite as the shelf space at Amazon or eBay. But while there may be infinite typewriters, there is a scarcity of talent, expertise, experience, and mastery in any given field. Finding and nurturing true talent in a sea of amateurs may be the real challenge in today's Web 2.0 world. The fact is, Anderson's vision of a hitless, flattened media is a self-fulfilling prophecy. Without the nurturing of talent, there will, indeed, be no more hits, as the talent that creates them is never nourished or permitted to shine.

Today, on a Web where everyone has an equal voice, the words of the wise man count for no more than the mutterings of a fool. Sure, all of us have opinions; but as I discuss more fully in Chapter 2, few of us have special training, knowledge, or hands-on experience to generate any kind of real perspective. Thomas Friedman, the *New York Times* columnist, and Robert Fisk, the Middle Eastern correspondent of the *Independent* newspaper, for example, didn't hatch from some obscure blog—they acquired their in-depth knowledge of the Middle East by spending years in the region. This involved considerable investments of time and resources, for which both the journalists themselves, and the newspapers they work for, deserve to be remunerated.

Talent, as ever, is a limited resource, the needle in today's digital haystack. You won't find the talented, trained individual shipwrecked in his pajamas behind a computer, churning out inane blog postings or anonymous movie reviews. Nurturing talent requires work, capital, expertise, investment. It requires the complex infrastructure of traditional media—the scouts, the agents, the editors, the publicists, the technicians, the marketers. Talent is built by the intermediaries. If you "disintermediate" these layers, then you do away with the development of talent, too.

The economics of *The Long Tail* are dead wrong. Technology utopians like Anderson suggest that self-created content will somehow result in an endless village of buyers and sellers, each buying a little and choosing from an extraordinary number of things. But the more self-created content that gets dumped onto the Internet, the harder it becomes to distinguish the good from the bad—and to make money on any of it. As Trevor Butterworth reported in the *Financial Times,* nobody is getting rich from blogging, not even Markos Moulitsas Zuniga, the founder of the Daily Kos, the most popular of all the political blogs.

Take the case of GoFugYourself.com, a celebrity parody site attracting a huge audience of 100,000 visitors a day. According to Butterworth, the site is only generating "beer money" for its founders. Above-average sites like JazzHouston.com, which attracts 12,000 visitors a day, bring in peanuts—around $1,000 a year in ad revenue from Google.[10] Then there's Guy Kawasaki, author of one of the fifty most popular blogs on the Internet, whose pages were viewed almost two and a half million times in 2006. And how much did Kawasaki earn in ad revenue in 2006 off this hot media property? Just $3,350.[11] If this is Anderson's long tail, it is a tail that offers no one a job.

At best, it will provide the monkeys with peanuts and beer.

The real challenge in Anderson's long tail market of infinite shelf space is finding what to read, listen to, or watch. If you think the choice in your local record store is daunting, then just wait till the long tail uncoils its infinite length. Trawling through the blogosphere, or the millions of bands on MySpace, or the tens of millions of videos on YouTube for the one or two blogs or songs or videos with real value isn't viable for those of us with a life or a full-time job. The one resource that is challenged all the more by this long tail of amateur content is our time—the most limited and precious resource of all.

Yes, a number of Web 2.0 start-ups such as Pandora. com, Goombah.com, and Moodlogic.com are building artificially intelligent engines that supposedly can automatically tell us what music or movies we will like. But artificial intelligence is a poor substitute for taste. No software can replace the implicit trust we place in a movie review by Nigel Andrews (*Financial Times*), A. O. Scott (*New York Times*), Anthony Lane (*New Yorker*), or Roger Ebert (*Chicago Sun-Times*)—a thoughtfully crafted review, informed by decades of education, training, and movie-reviewing experience. No algorithm can match the literary analysis of the reviewers at the *London* or the *New York Review of Books,* nor the wealth of musical knowledge espoused by reviewers at magazines like *Rolling Stone, Jazziz,* or *Gramophone.*

Chris Anderson is right to say the infinite space of the Internet will afford more and more opportunities for niche programming, but the downside is that this will ensure that such niches generate less and less revenue. The more specialized the niche, the narrower the market. The narrower the market, the more shoestring the production budget, which compromises the quality of the programming, further reducing the audience and alienating the advertisers.

One example of this dark cycle is NBC's attempt in 2006 to create exclusive interactive Internet mini-episodes of the sitcom *The Office*. The mini-episodes were so underfunded that NBC couldn't even afford to cast Steve Carell, the star of show. As one TV critic said, it looked like "outtakes swept up from the remainder bin."[12]

Network television is already grappling with the fragmentation of the audience into thinner and thinner slices. In 2006, NBC developed video sites for gay men and TV junkies, and CBS introduced an interactive Web channel for teenagers and another (Showbuzz.com) dedicated to entertainment news and gossip. The Scripps Network, in a desperate attempt to expand its total viewership, also introduced video channels for increasingly narrow subjects, from woodworking to quilting to healthy eating.

Where does it end? With a channel for every one of us, in which we are the solitary broadcaster and the sole audience? This would be democratization on the most fundamental level. Such an absurd conclusion is not pure fantasy. In the short time since FOO Camp 2004, Web 2.0's narcissistic, self-congratulatory, self-generated content revolution has exploded. Before September 2004, there was no YouTube, and author-generated sites like Wikipedia and MySpace were well-kept Silicon Valley secrets. Today, we are watching a hundred million clips a day on YouTube, and MySpace, founded in July 2003, has over ninety-eight million profiles. There are now almost infinite social media sites for teens, pre-teens, post-teens, and, as we will see, even fake teens.

The bloggers and the podcasters have taken over our computers, our Internet-enabled cell phones, our iPods. What was once just a weird Silicon Valley cult is now transforming America.

In a cartoon that appeared in *The New Yorker* in 1993, two dogs sit beside a computer. One has his paw on the keyboard; the other is looking up at him quizzically.

"On the Internet," the dog using the keyboard reassures his canine friend, "nobody knows you're a Dog."

That is more true than ever. On today's self-publishing Internet, nobody knows if you're a dog, a monkey, or the Easter Bunny. That's because everyone else is too busy ego-casting, too immersed in the Darwinian struggle for mind-share, to listen to anyone else.

But we can't blame this sad state of affairs on some other species. We human beings hog the limelight on this new stage of democratized media. We are simultaneously its amateur writers, its amateur producers, its amateur technicians, and, yes, its amateur audience.

Amateur hour has arrived, and the audience is now running the show.

2

the noble amateur

Every revolution is celebrated on behalf of some seemingly noble abstraction. And the Web 2.0 revolution is no different. The noble abstraction behind the digital revolution is that of the *noble amateur*.

I first heard this phrase in 2004, over breakfast with a Friend of O'Reilly. He had told me that these "noble amateurs" would democratize what, with a wave of his coffee cup, he called "the dictatorship of expertise." The Web 2.0 was the most "awesomely" democratic consequence of the digital revolution, he said. It would change the world forever.

"So instead of a dictatorship of experts, we'll have a dictatorship of idiots," I might have responded. His ideal of the "noble amateur" seemed like more Silicon Valley chatter, just more irrationally exuberant nonsense.

But the ideal of the noble amateur is no laughing matter. I believe it lies at the heart of Web 2.0's cultural revolution and threatens to turn our intellectual traditions and institutions upside down. In one sense, it is a digitalized version of Rousseau's noble savage, representing the triumph of innocence over experience, of romanticism over the commonsense wisdom of the Enlightenment.

So let me begin this journey to the center of the digital world with a definition. The traditional meaning of the word "amateur" is very clear. An amateur is a hobbyist, knowledgeable or otherwise, someone who does not make a living from his or her field of interest, a layperson, lacking credentials, a dabbler. George Bernard Shaw once said, "Hell is full of amateur musicians," but that was before Web 2.0. Today, Shaw's hell would have broadband access and would be overrun with bloggers and podcasters.

For a more empirical and objective definition, the *Shorter Oxford English Dictionary (OED)* defines "amateur" as:

> 1. A person who is fond of something; a person who has a taste for something   2. A person who practices something, esp. an art or game, only as a pastime; an unpaid player, performer (opp. *professional*), also (*depreciative*) a dabbler

The *Shorter OED*, of course, epitomizes what the friend of O'Reilly would call the "dictatorship of expertise." Published by Oxford University Press and currently in its fifth edition, the *Shorter OED* is a two-volume, four-thousand-page dictionary edited by a team of sixteen professional lexicographers and an expert cohort of other researchers and advisors. It is a book in which two plus two always adds up to four.

On today's Internet, however, amateurism, rather than expertise, is celebrated, even revered. Today, the *OED* and the *Encyclopaedia Britannica*, two trusted reference volumes upon which we have long relied for information, are being replaced by Wikipedia and other user-generated resources. The professional is being replaced by the amateur, the lexicographer by the layperson, the Harvard professor by the unschooled populace.

Wikipedia describes itself as "the free encyclopedia that anyone can edit." The site claims to run on "democratic" principles, as its two hundred thousand anonymous editors are all unpaid volunteers. Unlike the *OED*, which was crafted by a carefully vetted and selected team of experienced professionals, Wikipedia, as I discussed earlier, allows absolutely anyone to add and edit entries on its Web site.

So what is wrong with such a "democratized" system? Isn't the ideal of democracy that everyone has a voice? Isn't that what makes America so attractive? (While not born in the United States myself, I've lived here since the early 1980s, am married to a woman from Alabama, and have raised my family in California. I'm a classic example of the immigrant entrepreneur who came to America seeking more economic and cultural freedom.)

While this is true in terms of elections, a radically democratic culture is hardly conducive to scholarship or to the creation of wisdom. The reality is that we now live in a highly specialized society, where excellence is rewarded and where professionals receive years of training to properly do their jobs, whether as doctors or journalists, environmental scientists or clothing designers. In *The Wealth of Nations,* economist Adam Smith reminds us that specialization and division of labor is, in fact, the most revolutionary achievement of capitalism:

> The greatest improvement in the productive powers of labour, and the greater part of the skill, dexterity, and judgment with which it is any where directed, or applied, seem to have been the effects of labour.

In the twenty-first century, this division of labor does not just refer to the breakdown of jobs in a manufacturing plant or on an assembly line. It includes the labor of those who choose a trade or a field, acquire education or training, gain experience, and develop their abilities within a complex meritocracy. They all have the same goal: to acquire expertise.

In a notorious section from *The German Ideology,* Karl Marx tried to seduce his reader with an idyllic post-capitalist world where everyone can "hunt in the morning, fish in the afternoon, rear cattle in the evening, criticize after dinner." But if we can all simultaneously be hunters, fishers, cattle herders, and critics, can any of us actually excel at anything, whether hunting, fishing, herding, or criticizing? In a world in which we are all amateurs, there are no experts.

On the Web 2.0, one senses that is perhaps the ideal. Wikipedia's entry for the word "amateur"—which has been amended by other editors more than fifty times since June 2001—defines one as both a "virtuoso" and a "connoisseur":

> In the areas of computer programming and open source, as well as astronomy and ornithology, many amateurs make very meaningful contributions equivalent to or exceeding those of the professionals. To many, description as an amateur is losing its negative meaning, and actually carries a badge of honor.

While the Wikipedia entry doesn't use the word "noble," you don't need to be a scholar to read between the lines. The editors at Wikipedia wear their amateur badge with pride. The problem? As Marshall Poe put it in a recent conversation:

> It's not exactly expert knowledge; it's common knowledge . . . when you go to nuclear reactor on Wikipedia you're not getting an encyclopedia entry, so much as you're getting what people who know a little about nuclear reactors know about nuclear reactors and what they think common people can understand. [Wikipedia] constantly throws

people off and they think, well, if it's an encyclopedia why can't I cite it; why can't I . . . rely on it?
And you can't; you just can't rely on it like that.[1]

Wikipedia's editors embrace and revel in the common-
ness of their knowledge. But as the adage goes, a little
knowledge is a dangerous thing. Because on Wikipedia,
two plus two sometimes *does* equal five.

In the July 2006 issue of *The New Yorker*, Stacy Schiff
wrote, "Wikipedia may be the word's most ambitious vanity press."[2] But it is a press with a peculiar sort of vanity,
raising up the amateur to a position of prominence
exceeding that of the salaried experts who do what they
do for money. Wikipedia claims to be amassing the world's
largest real estate of knowledge, and yet Wikipedia's readers seem to revel in its very lack of authority.

This vanity of the innocent was underscored by founder
Jimmy Wales, who, commenting about the identity of
Wikipedian editors, said, "To me, the key thing is getting
it right. I don't care if they're a high school kid or a Harvard professor." Or, it seems, a high school kid *posing* as a
Harvard professor. In fact, in March 2007, *The New Yorker*
magazine discovered that "Essjay," an avid Wikipedia
contributor interviewed for a recent article by the magazine's Stacey Schiff, had edited thousands of Wikipedia
articles under a false identity. It turned out that "Essjay"
was not a tenured professor of theology with four academic degrees, as his profile claimed, but was in fact a
twenty-four-year-old high school graduate from Kentucky

named Ryan Jordan with no academic or professional credentials. What's worse is that when confronted with the blatant deception perpetrated by one of his star contributors ("Essjay" was not only a frequent editor of articles but also had administrative privileges on Wikipedia and had recently been given a job at the for-profit company Wikia, which Wales also helped to found), Wales was less than apologetic. "I regard it as a pseudonym and I don't really have a problem with it," he told *The New Yorker.*

Wales is himself a graduate school drop-out from both the University of Alabama and Indiana University.[3] The problem is, how does Wales know who's right? Often, you need an expert to help you figure it out.

Wales told *The New Yorker*'s Schiff, "I'm actually quite an enlightenment kind of guy." But the reverse is actually true—he's a *counter*-enlightenment guy, a wide-eyed romantic, seducing us with the ideal of the noble amateur. So who is Jimmy Wales? Educated in a one-room school in Huntsville, Alabama, Wales first discovered the Internet as a teenager playing Multi-User Dungeon (MUD) fantasy games such as Zork, Myst, and the Scepter of Goth. Then, as an undergraduate at the University of Alabama, Wales was converted by the libertarian idealism espoused by Ayn Rand, a philosophy of rugged self-realization, which stands against tradition and established authority.

In the Wild West–style Internet economy of the mid-Nineties, Wales co-founded a Web directory called Bomis. Described by *The Atlantic* magazine as "The *Playboy* of the Internet," Bomis provided the peer-to-peer technology to link together sites about Pamela Anderson and Anna Kournikova. What Wales had learned as an adolescent playing video games, and relearned from his experience with Bomis, was the power of the network, the value of what has become known as "distributed" technology. In January 2000, he hired Larry Sanger, a doctoral student in philosophy, with the instruction of building an open-source encyclopedia project. This blossomed into Nupedia, a free encyclopedia consisting of peer-reviewed articles by experts and scholars. However, while many experts embraced Nupedia, the site was rejected by digital utopians because its strict editorial standards went against their "democratic" principles. So, a year later, Wales and Sanger added wiki technology, which allows anyone to add content to a communal Web site without the approval of a central authority.[4] The hubris behind this experiment would later grow into the idea that a collective of anonymous, volunteer enthusiasts could aggregate their knowledge into the sum total of human wisdom.

As a result, in the not-so-hidden ideology of the collective Wikipedia experiment, the voice of a high school kid has equal value to that of an Ivy League scholar or a trained professional. This became Jimmy Wales' big idea. Wales, who was lauded on *Time* magazine's 2006 list of Top 100 People Who Shape Our World as a "champion of internet egalitarianism," believes that the expert is born rather than bred and that talent can be found in the most unexpected places. It is a metaphysical conceit that can be traced back to his libertarian roots. To Wales, neither our reputations nor our qualifications have any intrinsic value. In his ideal world, everyone should be given equal voice, irrespective of their title, knowledge, or intellectual or scholarly achievements.

Jimmy Wales and Larry Sanger launched Wikipedia in January 2001. "Humor me," Larry Sanger wrote to all his friends. "Go there and add a little article. It will take all of five or ten minutes." Well, millions of amateur Wikipedians have humored Sanger and Wales more than they could ever have imagined. But in the cult of the amateur, those who know most can be persecuted by those who know the least.

Dr. William Connolley, a climate modeler at the British Antarctic Survey in Cambridge and an expert on global warming with many professional publications to his credit, recently went head-to-head with a particularly aggressive Wikipedia editor over the site's global warming entry, when, after trying to correct inaccuracies he noticed in the entry, he was accused of "strongly pushing his POV [point of view] with systematic removal of any POV which does not match his own."

Connolley, who was pushing no POV other than that of factual accuracy, was put on editorial parole by Wikipedia, and was limited to making one entry a day. When he challenged the case, the Wikipedia arbitration committee gave no weight to his expertise, treating Connelley, an international expert on global warming, with the same deference and level of credibility as his anonymous foe—who, for all anyone knew, could have been a penguin in the pay of ExxonMobil.

The consequences of this dismissal of traditional, credentialed experts on sites like Wikipedia are both chilling and absurd. Can a social worker in Des Moines really be considered credible in arguing with a trained physicist over string theory? Can a car mechanic have as knowledgeable a "POV" as that of a trained geneticist on the nature of hereditary diseases? Can we trust a religious fundamentalist to know more about the origins of mankind than a Ph.D. in evolutionary biology?

Unfortunately, the Web 2.0 revolution helps to foster such absurdities. By empowering the amateur, we are undermining the authority of the experts who contribute to a traditional resource like the *Encyclopaedia Britannica*—experts who, over the years, have included the likes of Albert Einstein, Marie Curie, and George Bernard Shaw. Indeed, what defines "the very best minds" available, whether they are cultural critics or scientific experts, is their ability to go beyond the "wisdom" of the crowd and mainstream public opinion and bestow on us the benefits of their hard-earned knowledge.

In undermining the expert, the ubiquity of free, user-generated content threatens the very core of our professional institutions. Jimmy Wales' Wikipedia, with its millions of amateur editors and unreliable content, is the seventeenth most-trafficked site on the Internet; Britannica.com, with its 100 Nobel Prize winners and 4,000 expert contributors, is ranked 5,128.

Fighting against free is hard, if not impossible. The current Britannica company, for example, employs over a hundred professional editors and fact-checkers, and pays its 4,000 contributors. Wikipedia, in contrast, pays for none of its content and employs only a handful of paid employees. The 232-year-old Britannica went through a series of painful layoffs in 2001 and 2002, cutting its 300-person staff in the United States almost by half; with the advent of Wikipedia, no doubt more layoffs are to come.[5]

So what do we get in exchange for free amateur content? We get, of course, what we pay for. We get what the great thinker and writer Lewis Mumford called "a state of intellectual enervation and depletion hardly to be distinguished from massive ignorance." Today's editors, technicians, and cultural gatekeepers—the experts across an array of fields—are necessary to help us to sift through what's important and what's not, what is credible from what is unreliable, what is worth spending our time on as opposed to the white noise that can be safely ignored. So while the professionals—the editors, the scholars, the publishers—are certainly the victims of an Internet that diminishes their value and takes away their jobs, the greater victims of all this are *us*, the readers of Wikipedia and of the blogs and all the "free" content that is insistently reaching out for our attention. And when misinformation is spread, it is we the people who suffer the consequences. For the sad fact is that while Dr. William Connolley may be able to discern the misinformed ravings of moonbats (a term Eric Raymond, a respected open-source pioneer, used to describe the

Wikipedia community) from the wisdom of experts, the average Internet user cannot. Most of us assume that the information we take in can be trusted.

But when the information is created by amateurs, it rarely can be. And the irony in all this is that democratized media will eventually force all of us to become amateur critics and editors ourselves. With more and more of the information online unedited, unverified, and unsubstantiated, we will have no choice but to read everything with a skeptical eye. (That is why, in February 2007, the Middlebury College history department banned students from citing Wikipedia as a source for research papers.) The free information really isn't free; we all end up paying for it one way or another with the most valuable resource of all—our time.

Citizen Journalists

Wikipedia is far from alone in its celebration of the amateur. The "citizen journalists," too—the amateur pundits, reporters, writers, commentators, and critics on the blogosphere—carry the banner of the noble amateur on Web 2.0. In fact, citizen journalism is a euphemism for what you or I might call "journalism by nonjournalists," or as Nicholas Lemann, Dean of the Columbia University Graduate School of Journalism,[6] described them in *The New Yorker:* people who are not employed by a news organization but perform a similar function. Professional journalists acquire their craft through education and through the firsthand experience of reporting and editing the news under the careful eye of other professionals. In contrast, citizen journalists have no formal training or expertise, yet they routinely offer up opinion as fact, rumor as reportage, and innuendo as information. On the blogosphere, publishing one's own "journalism" is free, effortless, and unencumbered by pesky ethical restraints or bothersome editorial boards.

The simple ownership of a computer and an Internet connection doesn't transform one into a serious journalist any more than having access to a kitchen makes one into a serious cook. But millions of amateur journalists think that it does. According to a June 2006 study by the Pew Internet and American Life Project, 34 percent of the 12 million bloggers in America consider their online "work" to be a form of journalism.[7] That adds up to millions of unskilled, untrained, unpaid, unknown "journalists"—a thousandfold growth between 1996 and 2006—spewing their (mis)information out in the cyberworld.

Most amateur journalists are wannabe Matt Drudges— a pajama army of mostly anonymous, self-referential writers who exist not to report news but to spread gossip, sensationalize political scandal, display embarrassing photos of public figures, and link to stories on imaginative topics such as UFO sightings or 9/11 conspiracy theories. Drudge, who once wrote that "the Net gives as much voice to a thirteen-year-old computer geek like me as to a CEO or speaker of the House. We all become equal,"[8] is the poster boy of the citizen journalist movement, flashing his badge of amateurism as a medieval crusader would wield a sword.

These four million wannabe Drudges revel in their amateurism with all the moral self-righteousness of religious warriors. They flaunt their lack of training and formal qualifications as evidence of their calling, their passion, and their selfless pursuit of the truth, claiming that their amateur status allows them to give us a less-biased, less-filtered picture of the world than we get from traditional news. In reality this is not so.

In 2005, in the aftermath of Hurricane Katrina, for example, many of the initial reports of the damage came from citizen journalists, people on the scene blogging about the chaos and taking photos of the devastation with their camera phones. But, as it turned out, these initial reports helped to spread unfounded rumors—inflated body counts and erroneous reports of rapes and gang violence in the Superdome—that were later debunked by the traditional news media. The most accurate and objective reports instead came from professional news reporters who brought us high-quality photographs of the disaster and information from key figures like the New Orleans police, rescue workers, the U.S. Army Corps of Engineers, as well as first-hand accounts from the citizens and victims themselves.

Citizen journalists simply don't have the resources to bring us reliable news. They lack not only expertise and training, but connections and access to information. After all, a CEO or political figure can stonewall the average citizen but would be a fool to refuse a call from a reporter or editor at the *Wall Street Journal* seeking a comment on a breaking story.

One leading champion of citizen journalism, Dan Gillmor, author of the crusading *We the Media: Grassroots Journalism by the People, for the People,* argues that the news should be a *conversation* among ordinary citizens rather than a lecture that we are expected to blindly accept as truth. But the responsibility of a journalist is to inform us, not to converse with us.

If you simply want to converse with a journalist, invite them to your local bar for a few drinks. That's exactly what I did in the fall of 2006 when I spent an evening with Al Saracevic, deputy business editor of the *San Francisco Chronicle.*

Halfway through the evening, we got onto the subject of amateur journalism. "So what do you think distinguishes bloggers from professional journalists?" I asked him.

I'd expected Saracevic to focus on the quality of the end product. I expected him to tell me that amateur reporting on recent events like the 7/6 London bombings or New Orleans after Katrina wasn't up to real journalistic standards because it wasn't vetted by knowledgeable editors or wasn't corroborated by multiple sources. But I was wrong. While Saracevic might have agreed with the above, he had something else on his mind.

"In America, bloggers don't go to jail for their work," he told me. "That's the difference between professionals and amateurs."[9]

Saracevic was referring to Lance Williams and Mark

Fainaru-Wada, his colleagues on the *Chronicle,* a two-person team of baseball reporters who had just been sentenced to eighteen months in prison for refusing to testify about the identity of the person who leaked them secret grand jury testimony from Barry Bonds.

In Saracevic's view, the blogosphere is a sideshow, all eyeballs and no real relevance, a poker game played with fake chips. Bloggers are very rarely sued or prosecuted because the government and corporations don't seem to really care what they write. As a result, they aren't held accountable for their work in the way that real reporters are.

In contrast, professional journalism matters. Companies sue newspapers, and reporters get sent to jail. Professional journalism is hardball. It counts—for the journalists, for corporations, for the government, and, most important, for all of us. This is because it is still only mainstream journalists and newspapers who have the organization, financial muscle, and credibility to gain access to sources and report the truth. As Saracevic later e-mailed me:

> It's as if libel law has taken a brief vacation so that citizen journalists can get their feet wet, while trashing the mainstream media for "not speaking truth to power," as Craig Newmark puts it. Well, speaking truth to power takes money. Money to pay lawyers. Lots and lots of lawyers. Say what you will about the mainstream media, it takes big companies with a

commitment to real investigative journalism to take
on big institutions with any hope of surviving.

Contrast this with another conversation I'd had, a few
months earlier, with Dan Gillmor, the champion of citizen journalism I introduced earlier. I'd asked Gillmor
what citizen journalism could provide that we can't get
from mainstream media.

Gillmor's answer reflected the self-absorption of the
typical amateur journalist. He told me that the real
value of citizen journalism was its ability to address
niche markets otherwise ignored by mainstream media.

When I asked him for an example, he replied, hybrid
cars. To him, proof of the value of citizen journalism
was in news blogs about the Toyota Prius. Leave wars to
the real reporters, he implied. The responsibility of
amateurs was to report the latest feedback about the
Prius. But is reporting about your favorite car really journalism? I asked him. According to Gillmor, it is.

> Is this journalism? I would say yes; it's a conversation, absolutely, but it's a collective bringing
> together of what people know, and when someone
> posts something that's not true, other people jump
> in and say well this is wrong.[10]

In other words, professional journalists can go to jail
for telling the truth; amateurs talk to each other about
their cars.

Unfortunately, the Internet is bloated with the hot air of these amateur journalists. Despite the size of their readership, even the A-List bloggers have no formal journalistic training. And, in fact, much of the real news their blogs contain has been lifted from (or aggregated from) the very news organizations they aim to replace.

It is not surprising then that these prominent bloggers have no professional training in the collection of news. After all, who needs a degree in journalism to post a hyperlink on a Web site? Markos Moulitsas Zuniga, for example, the founder of Daily Kos, a left-leaning site, came to political blogging via the technology industry and the military. Glenn Reynolds, who leans to the right, was a law professor and an amateur music producer before jumping on his digital soapbox. Drudge was a mediocre student who came to the media business via a job managing the CBS studio gift shop. Such amateurs treat blogging as a moral calling rather than a profession tempered by accepted standards; proud of their lack of training, standards, and ethical codes, they define themselves as the slayers of the media giants, as irreverent Davids overcoming the news-gathering industry Goliaths.

In the first Internet revolution, a Web site's value was determined by the number of eyeballs; in the Web 2.0 epoch, value is determined by its accumulation of amateur voices. In August 2006, I talked with digital media impresario Arianna Huffington (whose Huffington Post is one of the most highly trafficked blogs on the Internet), who boasted to me about ways in which her blog was planning to incorporate voices not traditionally heard in mainstream media. While papers like the *Los Angeles Times* or the *Washington Post* strive to maintain a singular, authoritative voice through the expert journalism they offer, Huffington claimed that her site was more truthful than traditional media because of its richer tapestry of amateur viewpoints. The problem is, these voices often distort the news, turning the music into noise (although as this book is going to press, Huffington is planning to add original reporting to her blog).

The New Yorker's Lemann points out that "societies create structures of authority for producing and distributing knowledge, information, and opinion."[11] Why? So that we know we can trust what we read. When an article runs under the banner of a respected newspaper, we know that it has been weighed by a team of seasoned editors with years of training, assigned to a qualified reporter, researched, fact-checked, edited, proofread, and backed by a trusted news organization vouching for its truthfulness and accuracy. Take those filters away, and we, the general public, are faced with the impossible task of sifting through and evaluating an endless sea of the muddled musings of amateurs.

Blogs on both the left and right have perfected the art of political extremism. Unlike professionally edited newspapers or magazines where the political slant of the paper is restricted to the op-ed page, the majority of blogs make radical, sweeping statements without evidence or substantiation. The most popular blogs are those that offer the seductive conspiracy theories and sensationalist antiestablishment platitudes that readers crave. As Lemann notes, even "the more ambitious blogs, taken together, function as a form of fast-moving, densely cross-referential pamphleteering—an open forum for every conceivable opinion that can't make its way into the big media, or . . . simply an individual's take on life."[12]

The downside of all this "democracy," which the *Washington Post*'s Robert Samuelson described as the "greatest outburst of mass exhibitionism in human history,"[13] is the integrity of our political discourse. Amateur journalism trivializes and corrupts serious debate. It is the greatest nightmare of political theorists through the ages, from Plato and Aristotle to Edmund Burke and Hannah Arendt—the degeneration of democracy into the rule of the mob and the rumor mill.

In 1961, Pulitzer Prize–winning playwright Arthur Miller wrote that "a good newspaper is a nation talking to itself." Fifty years later, in a nation where professional newspapers are losing readership to a seemingly endless stream of blogs and opinon-based sites, this conversation has taken a disturbing turn. Instead of starting our conversations about politics, economics, and foreign affairs from a common informed perspective, the amateur bloggers wax on trivial subjects like their favorite brand of breakfast cereal, or make of car, or reality television personality.

What Miller would see today in the Web 2.0 world is

a nation so digitally fragmented that it's no longer capable of informed debate. Instead, we use the Web to confirm our own partisan views and link to others with the same ideologies. Bloggers today are forming aggregated communities of like-minded amateur journalists—at Web sites like Townhall.com, HotSoup.com, and Pajamasmedia.com—where they congregate in self-congratulatory clusters. They are the digital equivalent of online gated communities where all the people have identical views and the whole conversation is mirrored in a way that is reassuringly familiar. It's a dangerous form of digital narcissism; the only conversations we want to hear are those with ourselves and those like us.

Recently, Jürgen Habermas, one of Europe's most influential social thinkers, spoke about the threat Web 2.0 poses to intellectual life in the West.

> The price we pay for the growth in egalitarianism offered by the Internet is the decentralized access to unedited stories. In this medium, contributions by intellectuals lose their power to create a focus.[14]

In this egalitarian environment, any intellectual—be it George Bernard Shaw, Ralph Waldo Emerson, or Habermas himself—is just another strident voice in the cacophony.

Not only can we now publish our own journalism, however substandard, we can self-publish our own literary works as well (I use the word "literary" loosely). Today's digital print-on-demand services are turning amateur novelists into modern-day Gutenbergs, enabling anyone to publish anything, regardless of quality, for a fee. Blurb.com, for example, sells a self-publishing technology that enables unpublished writers, photographers, and bloggers to transform their online blogs into physical books. With Lulu, another publish-on-demand service, all you have to do is upload your files, choose a binding and a cover, and a published book magically appears.

Blurb and Lulu are really just cheaper, more accessible versions of vanity presses, where the untalented go to purchase the veneer of publication. As of this date, Lulu has had little impact on professional book publishers. But whom are such sites benefiting? With 40,000 new books published each year by major houses—a number that most publishers would admit is far too many—do we really need to weed through the embarrassing efforts of hundreds of thousands of unpublished or self-published novelists, historians, and memoirists? According to John Sutherland, chairman of the 2005 Man Booker Prize committee, "It would take approximately 163 lifetimes to read all the fiction available, at the click of the mouse, from Amazon.com."[15] And these are just the professionally selected, edited, and published novels. Do we really need to wade though the tidal wave of amateurish work of authors who have never been professionally selected for publication?

The Liquid Library

Silicon Valley utopian Kevin Kelly wants to kill off the book entirely—as well as the intellectual property rights of writers and publishers. In fact, he wants to rewrite the very definition of the book, digitalizing all books into a single universal and open-source free hypertext—like a huge literary Wikipedia. In a May 2006 *New York Times Magazine* "manifesto," Kelly describes this as the "Liquid Version" of the book, a universal library in which "each book is cross-linked, clustered, cited, extracted, indexed, analyzed, annotated, remixed, reassembled, and woven deeper into the culture than ever before."[16] And Kelly couldn't care less whether the contributor to this hyper-textual utopia is Dostoyevsky or one of the seven dwarfs.

"Once digitized," Kelly says, "books can be unraveled into single pages or be reduced further, into snippets of a page. These snippets will be remixed into reordered books and virtual bookshelves." It is the digital equiva-lent of tearing out the pages of all the books in the world, shredding them line by line, and pasting them back together in infinite combinations. In his view, this results in "a web of names and a community of ideas."[17] In mine, it foretells the death of culture.

To anyone with the most elemental appreciation for the sanctity of the book and respect for the toils of the author, the implications of what Kelly suggests are, well, obscene. Is *Crime and Punishment* still *Crime and Punishment* if you remove the scene where Raskolnikov murders the pawnbroker? Should I be allowed to annotate and remix *Moby-Dick* so that Ahab spots the whale in the beginning of the journey? Is Plato's *Republic* still the same book if it contains a chapter from Locke and a paragraph from Kant? A finished book is not a box of Legos, to be recombined and reconstructed at whim.

Kelly's 2.0 vision may be the ultimate endpoint of the noble amateur. In his version of the future, individual writing will be freely distributed online. Writers will no longer receive royalties from their creative work, but will have to rely on speeches and selling add-ons to make a living.

The result: amateur writers and amateur content—all Drudge and no Dostoyevsky. Without a viable publishing business model, Kelly's universal library would degenerate into a universal vanity press—a hypertextual confusion of unedited, unreadable rubbish. Bookstores and publishing houses will disappear. All we will have left to read are our versions of our own stories.

In the music business, rock stars like Beck are singing the same tune as Kevin Kelly. Like Kelly and Jimmy Wales and the other Web 2.0 utopians, Beck is sold on the seductive nobility of the amateur. Beck's grand idea is to allow his fans to create personalized versions of his music—allowing them to design their own cover art, write their own lyrics, create their own electronic mixes. Beck would readily replace his own professional cover artists, lyricists, and recording engineers with the amateur enthusiast. As he told *Wired* magazine:

I'd love to put out an album that you could edit and mix and layer directly in iTunes. We did a remix project on a Web site a few years back where we put up the tracks on a song and let people make their own versions. There was something really inspiring about the variety and quality of the music that people gave back. In an ideal world, I'd find a way to let people truly interact with the records I put out—not just remix the songs, but maybe play them like a videogame.[18]

Similarly, the popular Toronto band Barenaked Ladies recently launched a "remix" contest, allowing fans to download songs from their latest album and re-mix and re-edit them into new versions, the best of which will eventually be released on CD. It's rather like an expert chef who, instead of cooking a fine meal, provides the raw ingredients for the diner. Or the surgeon who, instead of performing the surgery, leaves the amateur in the operating chamber with some surgical instruments and a brief pep talk.

As a profoundly unmusical music fan myself, I can scarcely conceive of Johann Bach releasing a raw version of his Brandenburg Concertos to be remixed or mashed up by his public. Or Mozart letting his listeners rewrite his operas and concertos. Can you imagine Bob Dylan releasing an interactive *Blood on the Tracks* that could be rearranged to sound like you? And once all of these amateur remixes and mash-ups end up on YouTube, as most ultimately do, it is us who are faced with the task of sitting through the millions of efforts to find the rare few that are worthwhile.

What the Web 2.0 gives us is an infinitely fragmented culture in which we are hopelessly lost as to how to focus our attention and spend our limited time. And this culture of the amateur goes far beyond books and music. Today, hundreds of thousands of amateur radio broadcasters or podcasters—would-be Howard Sterns and Rush Limbaughs—are using their computers to produce and distribute podcast shows. The latest fad—the new new thing—is video blogs, transforming anyone with a webcam and a microphone into instant stars on amateur video networks like YouTube and Bebo. What's next? Some believe we'll soon see the advent of "wiki-television," in which amateurs can submit content to be embedded in the story lines of their favorite television programs.

Broadcasting technology is becoming so pervasive that everything we do and say can, in a couple of clicks, be disseminated throughout the Internet. But is any of it worth watching?

A Burrito in Every Hand

The cult of the amateur even threatens the world of design, fashion, and advertising. In the October 2006 issue of *Fast Company* magazine, design maven Joe Duffy, founder of Duffy Designs, argued, in a debate with me about the democratization of the art of design, that anyone can and should be a designer. Joe Duffy argues that "the broader the participation in design, the more enthusiasm and demand for great design."[19] But to maintain their value, high-end clothing and cars and electronic equipment require not only great design and great engineering, but mystery and scarcity. What Duffy optimistically calls "participation in design," I argue, lessens the value of real innovation. Are great designs truly that easy to create? Today, the devil might wear Prada. But tomorrow, if Duffy gets his way, we may all be wearing self-designed Prada knockoffs.

Nevertheless, companies like Wal-Mart have begun to calculatingly play to our false assumptions about the "realness" of the amateur, getting free advertising in the process. In July 2006, untrained high school students were invited on Wal-Mart's "Hub" social network to create personalized video advertisements for the Arkansas retail giant. Cosponsored by Sony, the best of these "School My Way" amateur advertisements will be used in a Wal-Mart cable television commercial. It is yet another way in which the cult of the amateur is celebrated, even if it's only a marketing ploy. Companies have come to realize that not only is the amateur ad cheaper, but consumers have come to see it as rawer, less polished, and somehow more "real" or true than an ad prepared by a professional agency.

Nor is Wal-Mart alone. Nike, MasterCard, Toyota, and L'Oréal have run similar user-generated marketing contests, as have Cingular, Nestlé, and American Express. At the 2007 Super Bowl—one of the advertising industry's most important venues, which, with its audience of close to 100 million people, is known to be a showcase for the most creative and biggest-budget commercials,[20] Frito-Lay, Chevrolet, Diamond Foods, and the National Football League ran thirty-second commercials created by amateurs. The economics of these user-generated Super Bowl advertisements are particularly troubling. Take, for example, the competition that Frito-Lay ran to "discover" an amateur commercial for their Doritos corn chips. According to the American Association of Advertising Agencies, the average professionally produced thirty-second spot costs $381,000. Yet Frito-Lay paid a mere $10,000 to each of the five finalists in the competition, leaving $331,000 on the table. That's $331,000 that wasn't paid to professional filmmakers, scriptwriters, actors, and marketing companies—$331,000 sucked out of the economy.

A whole user-created "advertising platform" is even being pioneered by an Atlanta-based company called ViTrue, enabling consumers to create, produce, and upload their own video advertisements. One of ViTrue's early customers is the fast-growing restaurant franchise Moe's Southwest Grill, whose latest campaign to put a "Moe's Burrito in Every Hand" is being produced by amateur videographers (the creators of the best ad will receive Moe's burritos for life).

These campaigns manipulate our sensibility while undercutting the work of traditional advertising agencies and the talented people they employ. Unwittingly, we are giving away our time and our creative output to corporations like Wal-Mart or MasterCard in return for free burritos.

Becoming a doctor, a lawyer, a musician, a journalist, or an engineer requires a significant investment of one's life in education and training, countless auditions or entrance and certifying exams, and commitment to a career of hard work and long hours. A professional writer spends years mastering or refining his or her craft in an effort to be recognized by a seasoned universe of editors, agents, critics, and consumers, as someone worth reading and paying attention to. Those in the movie industry submit to long hours, harried schedules, and insane pressure to create a product that will generate profit in a business in which expenses are high and hits are unpredictable. Can the cult of the noble amateur really expect to bypass all this and do a better job?

Glenn Reynolds, the author of the Instapundit blog, claims that we are on the brink of the amateur century. Technology, Reynolds asserts, will give each individual the power only available traditionally to "nation-states, superheroes, or gods." We will, he argues, acquire the "intelligence of the gods" on everything from amateur journalism and music production to medicine, nanotechnology, and space travel.[21]

As we will see in the next chapter, this celebration of the amateur is having a corroding effect on the truth, accuracy, and reliability of the information we get. Think that's an exaggeration? Read on.

3

truth and lies

Not a day goes by without some new revelation that calls into question the reliability, accuracy, and truth of the information we get from the Internet. Sometimes it's a story about ads made to look like a personal page on social networks like MySpace or Facebook. Or a popular YouTube video that turns out to have been produced by a corporation with a vested interest in shaping consumers' opinions. Every week a new scandal further erodes our trust in the information we get from the Web.

In the digital world's never-ending stream of unfiltered, user-generated content, things are indeed often not what they seem. Without editors, fact-checkers, administrators, or regulators to monitor what is being posted, we have no one to vouch for the reliability or credibility of the content we read and see on sites like Xanga, Six Apart, Veoh, Yelp, Odeo, and countless others. There are no gatekeepers to filter truth from fiction, genuine content from advertising, legitimate information from errors or outright deceit. Who is to point out the lies on the blogosphere that attempt to rewrite our history and spread rumor as fact? When we are all authors, and some of us are writing fiction, whom can we trust?

Can You Believe It?

The September 2006 news clip on the German version of YouTube certainly looked genuine. It showed a professionally attired male news anchor seated at a wooden desk, with a map of Europe hanging behind him. It seemed to be a clip from *Tagesschau*—the most trusted news show in Germany. According to the anchor, the neo-Nazi NPD party had done well in the recent local elections:

> The NPD has received 7.3% of the votes in the German state of Mecklenburg-Western Pomerania—more than enough to enter the regional parliament.

Many German viewers were alarmed. Only those with the keenest of eyes could see that this YouTube video was not from the real *Tagesschau*—instead of the Das Erste studio logo, the top right-hand corner of the screen displayed the logo of a multi-spoked black sun that can be easily rearranged into three swastikas—the symbol that has been adopted by the German neo-Nazis.

Yes, the newscast, luckily, was a fraud. Made to look like a broadcast from the trusted Das Erste, this show was actually produced by the extremist neo-Nazi NPD as a trial run for a weekly Internet "news" show they were planning to launch as a vehicle for party propaganda and a tool for member recruitment.

Welcome to the truth, Web 2.0 style.

Things aren't much better on the American version of YouTube. During the November 2006 congressional elections, one of the most watched videos on YouTube was a campaign advertisement for Vernon Robinson, the Republican candidate for North Carolina's Thirteenth Congressional District.

The video was a distasteful attack on Brad Miller, Robinson's Democratic opponent. "Instead of spending money on cancer research, Brad Miller has spent your money to study the masturbation habits of old men," the commercial announced. "Brad Miller even spent your tax dollars to pay teenage girls to watch pornographic movies with probes connected to their genitalia!"

When criticized for mud-slinging, Vernon Robinson claimed that this video had never been approved for distribution. "We never put that out as an ad," he told Fox pundit Sean Hannity. "Someone put it on YouTube."

Is this a valid excuse for defamatory campaign tactics and blatant distortion of truth? In the Web 2.0 era, the

"Somebody put it on YouTube" excuse has become the equivalent of "the dog ate my homework."

Or what about Conrad Burns, the ex-senator from Montana, who lost the 2006 election against Democrat Jon Tester in part because of political propaganda spread on YouTube. In one popular video, Burns was shown falling asleep during a congressional hearing; in another he was captured on camera making a joke about the "nice little Guatemalan man" who did the gardening at his Virginia residence. And a third caught him warning his constituents about those who "drive taxicabs in the daytime and kill at night."

Given that Burns really did commit these gaffes, the videos weren't technically lies. But they weren't exactly truth either. Arrowhead77, the anonymous videographer who authored and posted the videos, was the pseudonym for a couple of Jon Tester's staffers. Between April and October 2006, a Tester aide, camcorder in hand, had gone on video safari, putting 16,000 miles on his car and following the Montanan senator on the campaign trail with his camera, ready to pounce at any slip of the tongue.

The problem is that the viral, editor-free nature of YouTube allows anyone—from neo-Nazis, to propagandists, to campaign staffers—to anonymously post deceptive, misleading, manipulative, or out-of-context videos. Conrad Burns was far from the only victim of this type of slander. In the 2006 Virginia senatorial race, the Democrats famously milked George Allen's *macaca* media moment to death. There are, no doubt, all sorts of wannabe Arrowhead77s out there, camcorders at the ready, preparing to big-game hunt Hillary Clinton, Rudy Giuliani, John McCain, and Barack Obama in the 2008 presidential campaign.

This is the future of politics in a Web 2.0 world. The supposed democratization medium of user-generated content is creating a tabloid-style gotcha culture—where one thoughtless throwaway remark overshadows an entire platform, and lifelong political careers are destroyed by an off-the-cuff joke at the end of a long campaign day.

And when information on politics and policy is so easily skewed or distorted, it's us, the electorate, who lose. When we, the citizens, don't know whom to believe or whom to trust, we may end up making the wrong decisions, or, worse yet, just switch off—from the candidates, from politics, from voting at all.

The YouTubification of politics is a threat to civic culture. It infantilizes the political process, silencing public discourse and leaving the future of the government up to thirty-second video clips shot by camcorder-wielding amateurs with political agendas.

The Truth About 9/11

In 2005, three young would-be filmmakers from the small town of Oneonta in upstate New York used two thousand dollars saved up from shifts at a Friendly's ice cream store to create an eighty-minute movie called *Loose Change*, a "documentary" (originally conceived as a fictional story) that claimed the 9/11 terrorist attacks were organized and carried out by the Bush administration. In a collage of out-of-context quotes and since-discredited news clips, the film painted a grossly distorted version of events. In this version, one of the Flight 11 hijackers was found alive after the crash, a few blocks from the Trade Center, and United Flight 93 didn't crash in a Pennsylvania field, but instead was redirected to Cleveland's Hopkins Airport. And the towers didn't collapse as a result of the impact from planes flown by Islamist suicide hijackers, but rather from the detonation of previously planted explosives. Originally posted on the Internet in the spring of 2005, *Loose Change* rose to the number-one spot on Google Video's "Top 100" by May 2006, generating ten million viewings in its first year alone.[1] That's ten million people being fundamentally misled about one of the most cataclysmic events in American history.

The "claims" made in *Loose Change* were completely discredited in the final report of the 9/11 Commission, a report that took two years to compile, cost $15 million, and was written by two governors, four congressmen, three former White House officials, and two special counsels. So whom do you trust? Three twenty-something amateurs with no college education or a team of experts that included America's brightest and most experienced elected officials and investigators? The Oneonta revisionists used the self-authoring technology of Web 2.0 to trash history about an event that cost thousands of

American lives, provoked a global backlash against Islam, and instigated two wars.

Yes, you could argue, to some people it was obvious the movie was a hoax. But how many other "hoaxes" are less obvious? How much of what we read or see on the Internet is equally deceptive? Is the person who posts an online ad or sends us a witty e-mail genuine, or is he or she a con artist, sexual predator, or hustler of one kind or another?

Scammers and Spammers

We've all received the e-mails from the Nigerian entrepreneur who promises us a million-dollar return on a "small" investment in his oil company, or the e-mails from an unknown address claiming to be from your credit card company asking you to verify your card number. Most of us know these are cons. But unfortunately, in an age the *New York Times* dubs Spam 2.0, digital scams are becoming harder and harder to spot.

One of the most persistent contemporary scams is called the "pump and dump," in which the perpetrators buy up penny stocks and then sell them, via spam, at artificially inflated prices. When the stock's price spikes a few days later, the spammers sell off their shares, receiving a 5 to 6 percent return and causing the values of the hoodwinked investors' shares to plummet.

Take, for example, a penny stock called the Diamant Art Corporation. At the end of the day on Friday,

December 15, 2006, this share was valued at 11 cents. Over that weekend, a botnet began "spewing out millions of spam messages" about the value of the shares. By Monday, many unsuspecting spam victims bought up shares, driving the price up to 19 cents, and finally peaking at 25 cents. Then, of course, the spammer sold off his shares at a huge profit. By Wednesday, December 20, the price was down to 12 cents.[2]

Or, in another popular con, spammers seize control of innocent computer networks, turning them into "botnets" by programming them to automatically send out spam that will then appear to be from a trustworthy source. Secure Computing, a leading Silicon Valley anti-spam company, has reported that 250,000 computers each day are transformed into botnets without their owner's knowledge.

Sex, Lies, and the Internet

In early September 2006, a Seattle-based techie named Jason Fortuny posted an ad under an invented female identity in the "casual encounters" section of Craigslist—the virtual marketplace for one-night stands and anonymous sex partners. Fortuny received 178 responses and proceeded to post them on his Web site—including the men's names, photos of them naked, even the identities of their wives. With the click of Fortuny's mouse, reputations were destroyed, careers ruined, marriages and families shattered, all for a petty prank. Yes, some of the victims were going behind their wives' backs, and perhaps they deserved what they got. But others were simply lonely people looking to make a connection.

This case underscores the dangers inherent in an editorless medium where the only rules are that there are no rules. With a few simple keystrokes, Fortuny was able to create a false identity and publish the fruits of his deceit to the world. Like too much of what is on the Web today, his prank was both dishonest and harmful. The irony of the case, of course, is that the very people who seek anonymity in the Web 2.0 were done in by it. The Web's cherished anonymity can be a weapon as well as a shield.

The fact is that rumors and lies disseminated online can tarnish reputations and ruin careers. In the summer of 2005, a woman named Julie posted a horrific tale on the Web site dontdatehimgirl.com, a message board that invites scorned women to vent about egregious behavior of ex-boyfriends. According to Julie's posting, a man named Guido had gotten her drunk earlier that summer, raped and sodomized her, infected her with a sexually transmitted disease, and left her so humiliated and depressed that she attempted suicide. This tragic story, accompanied by a photograph of the alleged offender, was viewed over 1,000 times, prompting one visitor to write, "This son of a bitch deserves to be in jail. We need to circulate his picture everywhere and let everyone know what he did."

Had the story been true, most of us would be inclined

to agree. The problem is, not a word of it was. "Guido" was actually Erik, a friend of "Julie" (shockingly, not her real name). She eventually admitted she had posted the sordid tale "as a joke."[3]

Where content is unvetted, no proof or evidence is required to back up one's claims (on dontdatehimgirl.com, users only have to check a box declaring the information to be truthful), and anonymous postings are allowed, wild exaggerations and fabrications are not uncommon. As "Julie" told the *Miami New Times*, "There is nothing to stop [someone] from slandering a guy with impunity. . . . I would guess the vast majority of the 'stories' posted are completely full of shit."

In traditional media, antidefamation and libel laws protect people from these kinds of vicious character assassinations. But due in part to the anonymity and casualness of most Web postings, these laws have been hard to enforce in the digital world. A Pennsylvania lawyer named Todd Hollis found messages on dontdatehimgirl.com accusing him of having herpes, being gay, and having knowingly spread a sexually transmitted disease. Hollis promptly sued the owner of the site, as well as the women who made the defamatory statements, for being "a secondary distributor of false information." But his effort to clear his name had some negative consequences. As a result of the publicity surrounding the suit, five more unflattering profiles of him were posted on the site; they have collectively been viewed over 50,000 times.[4]

Then there is Rafe Banks, an attorney who sued a former client for attacking him on his blog. The former client had a vendetta against Banks after Banks failed to refund a $3,000 fee, so he falsely accused Banks of bribing judges to dismiss charges against drug dealer clients, then threatened more accusations if Banks didn't pay up. Banks eventually won a settlement, but not before irreparable damage had been done to his professional reputation.[5]

The owners of traditional newspapers and news networks are held legally accountable for the statements of their reporters, anchors, and columnists, encouraging them to uphold a certain standard of truth in the content they allow in their paper or on their air. Web site owners, on the other hand, are not liable for what is posted by a third party. Some say that this is a protection of free speech. But at what cost? As long as the owners of Web sites and blogs are not held accountable, they have little encouragement or incentive to question or evaluate the information they post.

On the Web, rumors or misinformation from even a single source can spread with frightening speed. Take the experience of Amy Tan, the bestselling author of *The Joy Luck Club*. In an essay entitled "Personal Errata,"[6] she describes how erroneous facts about her career, background, and personal life, likely originating from a single posting, have multiplied in cyberspace to the point where they have become part of her official biography. According to online accounts, Tan attended eight different colleges, lived in a mansion in Silicon Valley, raised two children, has been married several times, and has won both a Pulitzer Prize and the Nobel Prize for literature. The real Amy Tan has, in fact, been married once, has no kids, lives in a San Francisco apartment, and has won neither prize (yet). With no one to step in and question the veracity of information in the digital world, mistakes, lies, and rumors multiply like germs.

Before the Web 2.0, our collective intellectual history has been one driven by the careful aggregation of truth—through professionally edited books and reference materials, newspapers, and radio and television. But as all information becomes digitalized and democratized, and is made universally and permanently available, the media of record becomes an Internet on which misinformation never goes away. As a result, our bank of collected information becomes infected by mistakes and fraud. Blogs are connected through a single link, or series of links, to countless other blogs, and MySpace pages are connected to countless other My Space pages, which link to countless YouTube videos, Wikipedia entries, and Web sites with various origins and purposes. It's impossible to stop the spread of misinformation, let alone identify its source. Future readers often inherit and repeat this misinformation, compounding the problem, creating a collective memory that is deeply flawed.

Lonely Girls and Sock Puppets

It's not just the information itself that we can no longer trust; with the anonymity that Web 2.0 technology affords, the sources of information are of unknown origin, and as we've seen, they often can't be trusted. The Internet is flooded with fake identities—fake bloggers, fake MySpace profiles, fake YouTube starlets, fake e-mail addresses, fake reviews on sites like Amazon (some of which clearly are the result of a personal vendetta). Fake identities on the Internet have, in fact, become so widely adopted, they've been given their own term: "sock puppet," meaning the alter ego through which one speaks on an online community or posts on a blog.

Two of the more well-known examples are a couple of puppets called Mikekoshi and sprezzatura. Mikekoshi—whose real name is Michael Hiltzik—is a Pulitzer Prize–winning journalist who, ironically enough, won his 1999 award for his reporting on corruption in the entertainment industry. Hiltzik, who up until April 2006 wrote the *Los Angeles Times'* "Golden State" blog, is a "strident liberal" frequently embroiled in polemical fireworks with conservative bloggers. But Hiltzik—whose tagline on his blog was "Michael Hiltzik on business, economics, and more with a California edge"—cheated. He invented an online identity called Mikekoshi, and then, under this moniker, aggressively defended his own work on his opponents' Web sites.

Lee Siegel, a senior editor at the *New Republic* magazine and the winner of the 2002 National Magazine Award for Reviews and Criticism, invented an online identity called "sprezzatura" (an Italian word meaning nonchalance), under which he harshly attacked the liberal media. Siegel went so far as to post explosive remarks by sprezzatura on his *own* blog. When accused of being sprezzatura, Siegel took his deception to the next level by categorically denying it.[7]

Hiltzik and Siegel were temporarily suspended from their respective publications for violating journalistic ethics by misrepresenting themselves online (the *Los Angeles Times* ethics guideline states that editors and reporters must identify themselves when dealing with the public) in a way that would never have been possible before the advent of 2.0 technologies. In traditional news media, there is no such thing as anonymity. Articles and op-eds run with bylines, holding reporters and contributors responsible for the content they create. This not only holds them to ethical standards, but also provides a level of assurance for the public; the writer is accountable for his or her reporting or opinions. If an op-ed writer works for a political party or a partisan think tank, for example, the reader is made aware of his or her affiliation and potential conflict of interest. If a reporter misrepresents himself, or misrepresents the facts, the infraction will be caught and he or she will be taken to task and possibly fired, as was the case with Jayson Blair of the *New York Times*. But in the anonymous world of the blogosphere, there are no such assurances, creating a crisis of trust and confidence.

Sock puppetry (both literal and figurative) is rampant on YouTube as well. In fact, the lies on YouTube are so well told that they have become detective stories in their own right. Take, for example, the famous story of YouTube's lonelygirl15, a sixteen-year-old who starred in a popular series of self-made YouTube videos chronicling the life of an angst-ridden and lonely teenage girl. Some viewers, over time, noticed that in places, the amateur lonelygirl15 videos appeared to have a professional hand behind them, raising questions about the girl's true identity. Soon the blogs were peppered with speculation. Some thought that YouTube itself might be producing the video to boost viewership. Other sleuths suspected the hand of the Beverly Hills–based talent agency Creative Artists Agency. Jon Fine of *BusinessWeek* wondered if it could have been something "dreamed up" by Scientologists, occultists, or some other obscure millenarian Christian sect.[8]

The question of the authenticity of the video became the story itself. Meanwhile, the audience grew and grew, and lonelygirl15 became YouTube's second-most-subscribed channel. None of her hundreds of thousands of viewers seemed to care whether they were watching sophisticated advertising or the musings of an angst-ridden teenager. Eventually, lonelygirl15's creators, a screenwriter and filmmaker from California, confessed: "Bree," the girl in the video, was, in fact, a twenty-something Australian actress named Jessica. The videos had been an experiment in what the creators called "a new art form"—scripted clips that they hoped to eventually turn into a movie.

But if we can't trust the authenticity of Bree's confessions—if her teenage angst is all a sham—then we've simply been hoodwinked. And it makes me wonder what else on YouTube, or in the blogosphere, is fiction or advertisement.

Howard Kurtz of the *Washington Post* summarized the farce of lonelygirl15 this way:

> The great thing about the Internet is that anyone, even a lonely 16-year-old girl, can record her thoughts and draw a big following. The maddening thing about the Internet is that she might not be lonely or 16.[9]

All this points to a fundamental flaw with our user-driven content. We're never sure if what we read or see is what it seems. The user-run Internet not only allows, but encourages, the invention of false identity. Yet no one questions why so many of us are determined to hide who we are or what our affiliation is. The problem for those of us who wish to know more about who we're communicating with is that, as Jack Shafer, media critic at Slate.com, says, "There are just too many places to hide now."

The Blogosphere and the Bazaar

Some argue that the Web 2.0, and the blogosphere in particular, represents a return to the vibrant democratic intellectual culture of the eighteenth-century London coffeehouse. But Samuel Johnson, Edmund Burke, and

James Boswell didn't hide behind aliases while debating one another. The fact is that too many of us aren't innately honest creatures, either on- or off-line. When a medium like the Web is unchecked by regulation or professional editors or filters, and when we're left to our own amateur devices, we don't always behave well.

Trust is the very foundation of any community. Every social contract theorist—from Hobbes and Locke to Jean-Jacques Rousseau—recognizes that there can be no peaceful political arrangement without a common pact. And, as anthropologist Ernest Gellner argues in his classic *Nations and Nationalism,* the core modern social contract is rooted in our common culture, in our language, and in our shared assumptions about the world. Modern man is socialized by what the anthropologist calls a common "high culture." Our community and cultural identity, Geller says, come from newspapers and magazines, television, books, and movies. Mainstream media provides us with common frames of reference, a common conversation, and common values.

Benedict Anderson, in *Imagined Communities,* explains that modern communities are established through the telling of common stories, the formation of communal myths, the shared sense of participating in the same daily narrative of life. If our national conversation is carried out by anonymous, self-obsessed people unwilling to reveal their real identities, then Anderson's imagined community degenerates into anarchy.

The Web 2.0 is exacerbating the disconnect between

truth and politics, too, if indeed there can ever be any absolute truth in politics.

The Web site Insight, for example, a remnant of a defunct print magazine owned by the Unification Church, caused a stir in January 2007 by publishing an erroneous story that the *New York Times* called the first anonymous smear of the 2008 presidential race. Insight posted a story—by an anonymous reporter citing anonymous sources—claiming that Senator Hillary Clinton's campaign was hatching a smear campaign against her rival for the Democratic nomination, Barack Obama. According to the Insight story, which was promptly discredited, the Clinton campaign was planning to accuse Obama of having been enrolled in an Islamic religious school in Indonesia as a child, and of having covered it up. Even though the report was denounced by both campaigns, uncorroborated by other news organizations, and unconfirmed by sources (because there were no identifiable sources), it was picked up by Fox News and was discussed extensively on the morning news programs and on conservative talk radio.

It is deeply disturbing that in our filter-free Web 2.0 world, rumors and lies concocted by anonymous (and no doubt amateur) reporters are lent legitimacy and propagated by mainstream media channels. As Ralph Whitehead Jr., a professor of journalism at the University of Massachusetts, told the *New York Times*, "If you want to talk about a business model that is designed to manufacture mischief in large volume, that would be it."

When Charles Johnson, a rabidly pro-Israeli blogger at Little Green Footballs, discovered a doctored photo of a war scene in Beirut from a Reuters photographer named Adnan Hajj, tens of thousands concluded that the whole mainstream media was pro-Hezbollah, pro-Syria, and pro-terrorist. What the Reuters reporter did—staging and manipulating a photograph in order to create a more dramatic image—was a travesty; it utterly violated our expectations of truth and objectivity in journalism. And as a representative of a trusted, 155-year-old news organization, Hajj was duly excoriated for it. Following Reuters' immediate investigation of the matter, both Hajj and his editor were fired, and all 920 photos Hajj had taken in his career at Reuters were removed from the Web site. Reuters even went one step further to prevent such breaches in the future, by requiring all staff and freelance photographers to sign an enhanced code of ethical conduct.[10]

In contrast, on YouTube, one can watch thousands of short videos of grieving Lebanese men and women in the ruins of Beirut, holding dead babies in their arms. On a Web site with no filters, no ethical codes, no accountability or disciplinary consequences, one has no way of knowing how many of these films were doctored. As the *Washington Post* concluded, YouTube is a "video Dumpster" for a "disorganized bazaar of images."[11] For every Adnan Hajj in the mainstream media, there are hundreds of amateur polemicists peddling their propaganda and distortions on the Web.

In fact, the Web 2.0 media has put the horse before the cart—the new information disseminated on it is endless and mind-numbing. What is in short supply is reasoned, informed analysis. All the raw sensationalized information in the YouTube Dumpster—whether or not it is genuine—has no real value without expert interpretation and commentary. A photograph of a dead Lebanese or Israeli baby is not a helpful guide to understanding the complex situation of the Middle Eastern conflict.

In the golden age of media, revered journalists like Edward R. Murrow and Walter Cronkite were cultural heroes—universally admired, trusted, and respected. But in today's world, they would be C-list celebrities, as fewer and fewer of us pay any attention to the traditional news media. Instead, many of us—especially younger Americans—get our own, personalized version of the news at sites like Instapundit.com or at the Daily Kos, where we can be sure that the prevailing sentiment matches our own. Wittingly or not, we seek out the information that mirrors back our own biases and opinions and conforms with our distorted versions of reality. We lose that common conversation or informed debate over our mutually agreed-upon facts. Rather, we perpetuate one anothers' biases. The common community is increasingly shattering into three hundred million narrow, personalized points of view. Many of us have strong opinions, yet most of us are profoundly uninformed.

Library of Babel

In 1939, Jorge Luis Borges, a half-blind Argentine from Buenos Aires with a genius for dark literary fantasy, wrote a short essay called "The Total Library," predicting the horrors of the infinite library, one that has no center, no logic. Instead, it is a chaos of information, "composed of an indefinite and perhaps infinite number of hexagonal galleries."

Borges' "The Total Library" is today's Internet—anonymous, incorrect, chaotic, and overpowering. It is a place where there is no concrete reality, no right and wrong, no governing moral code. It is a place where truth is selective and constantly subject to change. The experience of surfing the Internet is akin to wandering around the hexagonal galleries of Borges' Library of Babel. Truth is elusive, always one click or Web site away.

Even conventional blogs aren't always what they seem to be. They can be faked, hidden, or hacked. They can become the tools of corporations, political propagandists, or identity thieves. The newest phenomenon on the Web are "splogs"—a combination of spam and blogs. Generated from software that allows users to create thousands of blogs per hour, splogs are fake blogs designed to mirror the real blogs in a sneaky ploy to trick advertisers and search engines and drive traffic and thus pay-per-click revenue. According to a researcher at the University of Maryland, splogs make up 56 percent of active blogs, clogging up the blogosphere with some 900,000 posts a day. Dave Sifry, the CEO of Technorati, the dominant search engine that indexes blogs, believes that splogs make up 90 percent of new blogs. As the September 2006 issue of *Wired* magazine noted, these sploggers "build entire online ecosystems of sleaze, twaddle, and gobbledygook," designed to waste the time of Internet users and steal revenue from innocent advertisers.[12]

A first cousin of splogs are flogs. Floggers are bloggers who claim to be independent but are actually in the pay of a sponsor, like the three Edelman PR staffers who, in 2006, attacked Wal-Mart critics while posing as grass-roots "Working Families for Wal-Mart" bloggers. Wal-Mart's commercial relationship with Edelman PR was not something, of course, that these floggers wrote about on their flogs.

PayPerPost.com, a Web 2.0 start-up backed by respected Silicon Valley venture capital firm Draper Fisher Jurvetson, acts as middleman between advertisers and floggers, paying floggers anything from $5 to $10 per post. PayPerPost.com calls itself a "marketplace for Consumer Generated Advertising." More accurately, it's a dark alleyway on the Internet where bloggers sell their souls to the highest bidder.

It may surprise you to know that advertisers, too, are victims. As much as we may focus on the way in which they deceive us, they, too, it turns out, are being deceived. In 2006, the professional monitoring service Click Forensic proved that at least 14 percent of the advertisements sold by search engines are bogus clicks, generating a payment for the search company without creating any real advertising value in return.[13]

In fact, a whole underground network of "domain parking" sites consisting solely of links and recycled banner ads has risen up, existing strictly to generate more clicks for which advertisers can be billed. And click-fraud scams are growing in both scope and number. In some, "paid to read" rings, often with hundreds or thousands of members scattered all over the world, are paid to sit at their computers and click over and over on a link. In others, automated programs called "clickbots" generate high volumes of anonymous, bogus clicks that are harder to track down than manual clicks. The result is that businesses, which pay per click on their ads, dole out huge, inflated sums to advertising companies for clicks that generate no returns in sales, customers, or genuine "stickiness."

The Atlanta-based company MostChoice.com was one such victim. In 2006, the company's founder, Martin Fleishman, noticed a growing number of clicks from places like South Korea and Syria—particularly puzzling since MostChoice serves mostly U.S.-based customers. After hiring a programmer to design a system that could analyze the length and origin of every click on a company ad, he discovered that most questionable clickers had left the site in a matter of seconds, and that none of those clicks had resulted in any new clients or business. Indeed, he had fallen prey to an elaborate click-fraud scheme— one that had cost his company over $100,000 in fruitless advertising fees. And this case is far from an anomaly. Click fraud, which, according to *The Economist* magazine, made up somewhere between 10 percent and 50 percent of all online advertising in 2006—adding up to between $3 billion and $13 billion—is perhaps the single biggest threat to the viability of the advertising-centric Web 2.0 economy. It makes Enron look like a rounding error.[14]

From splogs and flogs to botnets and clickbots, the Web 2.0 world has been invaded by liars, cheats, and fraudsters.

TiVo and Tea Parties

Before the Web 2.0, independent media content and paid advertising existed separately, in parallel, and were easily distinguishable from each other. On television and on the radio, commercials ran in thirty- or sixty-second slots, spaced predictably between every fifteen or so minutes of traditional programming. In newspapers and magazines, certain pages and columns were reserved for ads, and others were reserved for news and editorial content. Even in the first Internet revolution of the Nineties, content was separate from banner ads or interstitial paid advertisements. On the Web 2.0, that is no longer true. According to a Pew Internet and American Life Project study, while most people can distinguish between regular programming and infomercials on television, and between regular content and advertisements in print publications, 62 percent of Web browsers could not distinguish between paid and unpaid sites among search results.[15]

One reason for this is that new Web 2.0 technologies enable advertisers to transform what appears to be traditional content into commercials. Take a controversial new technology called "in-text" advertising, which allows companies like Microsoft and Target to sponsor keywords in traditional editorial articles so that when a reader moves their cursor over an underlined word, a pop-up ad appears. From the user's perspective, it's often not even clear what the association is between the underlined word and the advertisement. But from the advertiser's perspective, as long as they view the ad, it hardly matters.

This blurring of lines between advertising and content is partly due to our growing distrust in marketers and advertising. In January 2006, Edelman PR's "Trust Barometer" revealed a dramatic societal shift in whom we trust, from traditional media to trust in ourselves and our peers. In 2003, only 22 percent of American respondents reported trusting "a person like yourself or your peer." In January 2006, just three years into the Web 2.0 revolution, this had more than tripled, to 68 percent.[16]

As consumers, we have become increasingly suspicious of commercial messages, as well as increasingly intolerant of them. A 2005 report from the market research firm Yankelovich found that 69 percent of American consumers "were interested in ways to block, skip, or opt out of being exposed to advertising." As the editor of *PR Week* explained:

The past few years have seen something of a crisis in traditional TV and advertising, due in large part to two words that have only come into existence in the past half-decade or so: TiVo and blogs. These two phenomena have been the cornerstone of the shift in formula of most marketing programs away from the 30-second TV ad centerpiece toward a more fluid interaction with a highly knowledgeable audience.

The advertising industry certainly has gotten the message about "fluid" interactivity. In a much-quoted 2004 speech, James Stengel, Procter & Gamble's head of advertising, acknowledged that because today's consumers are "less responsive to messaging on traditional media," Web 2.0 consumers "are embracing new technologies that empower them with more control over how and when they are marketed to."

Given our mistrust of traditional commercials, the challenge for marketers in the Web 2.0 democratized media is to advertise without appearing to do so—by creating and placing commercial messages that appear to be genuine content. The challenge, and the opportunity, is to do this while building "authenticity"—authentic content, authentic brands, authentic commercial messages. But, of course, such authenticity is utterly contrived.

An executive at the Weber Shandwick PR agency described such strategies in *PR Week* as "seeding" the market with guerrilla publicity, product placement, and public relations stunts. The anonymous, editor-free Web 2.0 media provides an ideal environment for this, because if we don't know who produced an advertisement, we can be convinced that it was created by people "like us." Amateurism sells. The more unofficial the message, the more likely the consumer will take ownership of it.

Case in point? A short video called "Tea Partay" was posted on YouTube at the beginning of August 2006. Directed by Julien Christian Lutz, a music video veteran known as "Little X," "Tea Partay," a short rap video set on Cape Cod, which parodies the lifestyle of New England preppies, was viewed half a million times in the first couple of weeks of its YouTube release. But "Tea Partay" was not posted purely for our entertainment. In fact, it was paid for by Smirnoff to advertise a new malt drink called Raw Tea. Produced by the global advertising agency of Bartle Bogle Hegarty at a production cost of $200,000, it has proved to be one of the first big hits of viral advertising. And few consumers realized the extent to which they'd had the wool pulled over their eyes.

The beverage industry is not the only one to embrace guerrilla advertising. Nike ran a similarly successful video featuring the happy feet of Brazilian soccer star Ronaldinho as a promotion for its range of sports footwear. Other successful YouTube videos include Sony's "Colour Like No Other" spots, advertising its range of Bravia flat-screen TVs, and Volkswagen's "Unpimp Your Ride" features for their new GTI model. What is so disconcerting is that, to the uncritical eye, all these commercials appear to be entertainment. YouTube is a long commercial break dressed up as democratized media. It's the ultimate fantasy for the marketing and advertising industries.

As Chad Hurley, the founder of YouTube, told *Adweek:*

> We think there are better ways for people to engage with brands than forcing them to watch a commercial before seeing content. . . . We wanted to create a model where our users can engage with content and create a two-way communication between advertisers and users.

What Hurley is really suggesting is that on YouTube advertising and content can be successfully collapsed; that advertising is entertainment and entertainment is advertising. This "two-way communication" model has made YouTube into a grab bag of video commercials; everyone is using YouTube to peddle their brand.

What makes this deceptive to consumers is that YouTube's paid-for advertising appears no different from the rest of its content. In August 2006, the site began selling what it called "participatory video ads" (PVA), paid user-initiated spots that run on its front page. The first PVA was for a techno-dystopian movie called *Pulse,* and the ad was viewed 900,000 times over four days in August 2006.[17] The difference between the PVA and the standard YouTube content is virtually undetectable. And so is the distinction between participatory content and advertising on YouTube's "Brand Channels," which have been established solely to enable advertisers to sell products online. The first, paid for by Warner Brothers and dedicated to Paris Hilton's debut album *Paris*, was launched in the summer of 2006. With its Brand Channels, YouTube is turning itself into a democratized Shopping Network that does not distinguish between independent content and advertising.

But there *is* a fundamental difference between advertising and user-generated content—one is a paid message carefully calibrated to entice people to buy a product, while the other is an expression of information, creativity, or art. What happens to truth when politicians begin buying channels on YouTube to trash their opponents? And what becomes of artistic integrity when media companies use YouTube to broadcast "reviews" of their own products?

The irony of a "democratized" media is that some content producers have more power than others. In a media without gatekeepers, where one's real identity is often hidden or disguised, the truly empowered are the big companies with the huge advertising budgets. In theory, Web 2.0 gives amateurs a voice. But in reality it's often those with the loudest, most convincing message, and the most money to spread it, who are being heard.

The Wisdom of Crowds

In the Web 2.0 world, the crowd has become the authority on what is true and what is not. Search engines like

Google, which run on algorithms that rank results according to the number of previous searches, answer our search queries not with what is most true or most reliable, but merely what is most popular. As a result, our knowledge—about everything from politics, to current affairs, to literature, to science—is being shaped by nothing but the aggregation of responses. The search engine is a quantitative historical record of previous requests. So all the search engine offers is a ranking system that feeds back to us the wisdom of the crowd. In terms of links clicked on and sites visited, Google is an electronic mirror of ourselves.

But the problem is that the Web 2.0 generation is taking search-engine results as gospel. Imagine your child is doing a paper about the American presidency. He or she enters the words "White House" to learn more about the executive office, and decides to visit the links for the top three responses. Well, the third link in the Google search takes your kid to WhiteHouse.org—a spoof Web site that is dedicated to fake news, gossip, and offensive headlines.

And what's more, the Google search engine can be easily manipulated or corrupted. "Google bombing," which involves simply linking a large number of sites to a certain page, can raise the ranking of any given site in Google's search results. So anyone with a bit of tech savvy can rig the supposedly democratic Internet by repeatedly hyperlinking or cross-linking certain pages that they want to show up first in Google searches. These bombers are attempting to corrupt the collective "wisdom" stored in the Google algorithm.

Rather than user-generated content, what Google bombing represents is another kind of UGC—user-generated corruption. Google bombing has become a popular strategy for trying to sway popular opinion. In the 2006 congressional elections, for example, Google bombers at a liberal group blog called MyDD.com tried to discredit Republican senatorial candidate Jon Kyle by manipulating the algorithm so that when users searched for his name, a highly critical article published in the *Phoenix New Times* was among the first links to show up. And in a more humorous but no less agenda-pushing example of Google bombing, try entering the term "miserable failure" into Google and see what comes up.

"Social news" or "social bookmarking" sites like Digg, Reddit, Delicious, and the relaunched Netscape.com, which rely on the collective behavior of other users to prioritize the articles they display, also limit our access to fair and balanced information. These sites track the reading habits of their users and make recommendations based on aggregated preferences of the entire community. But such a method cannot be relied upon to keep us informed. When our individual intentions are left to the wisdom of the crowd, our access to information becomes narrowed, and as a result, our view of the world and our perception of truth becomes dangerously distorted.

For all their claims to be more democratic and honest, these supposedly editor-free social news sites are actually creating a more oligarchic and corrupt media. Social news sites such as Digg and Reddit are being manipulated by so-called "influencers"—people who artificially drive up the rankings of certain stories on these recommendation engines. According to the *Wall Street Journal*'s analysis of over 25,000 recommendations on six social sites, a tiny coterie of thirty users at Digg, a community of 900,000 users, were responsible for one-third of all front-page postings. And on Netscape.com, one user—with the screen name "Stoner"—was responsible for 217 (13%) of all the stories on the site's most popular list over a fourteen-day period. The *Wall Street Journal*'s research reveals that these sites reflect the preferences of the few rather than the "wisdom" of the masses.

The most disturbing thing of all about social news sites is that many influencers are gaming the engines to promote their own agendas. According to the *Wall Street Journal* report, some marketing companies are now selling "front-page exposure" on Digg. Others openly pay influencers to push stories. In October 2006, for example, User/Submitter.com began paying Digg users 10 cents for each story recommendation. And one seventeen-year-old Illinois high school senior, once ranked the number-two user on Digg, is now paid a monthly stipend of $1,000 by Netscape just to post his recommendations on the Netscape site.[18] Clearly, the wisdom of the crowd is an illusion—the anonymous influencers on Digg or Reddit are no more to be trusted than the anonymous amateur editors at Wikipedia or the anonymous amateur filmmakers on YouTube.

But even if there was such a thing as the wisdom of

the crowd, should we trust it? The answer, of course, is no. History has proven that the crowd is not often very wise. After all, many unwise ideas—slavery, infanticide, George W. Bush's war in Iraq, Britney Spears—have been extremely popular with the crowd. This is why the arbiters of truth should be the experts—those who speak from a place of knowledge and authority—not the winners of a popularity contest.

In 1841, a Scottish journalist called Charles Mackay wrote a classic critique of the irrational crowd called *Extraordinary Popular Delusions*.[19] Mackay used the Dutch Tulipmania fiasco and the South Sea Bubble to show that "whole communities suddenly fix their minds upon one object and go mad in its pursuit." If Mackay were around today, he would add Web 2.0 to the list of extraordinary popular delusions that have gripped the crowd. There is a twist, however, to today's grand digital delusion. With Web 2.0, the madness is about the crowd falling in love with itself.

Is that really the wisdom of the crowd?

4

the day the music died
[side a]

ARGEST RECORD STORE IN THE KNOWN
WORLD—OPEN NINE TO MIDNIGHT, 365 DAYS A
YEAR, read the sign outside the store on the corner
of Bay and Columbus in San Francisco.

Originally opened in April 1968, the store might not
have been as physically overwhelming as the Tower
Records that spanned three blocks in New York's Green-
wich Village, where the major music labels regularly
debuted new releases, or as rich in star sightings as the
Tower Records on Los Angeles' Sunset Strip, but to me it
was the *biggest* record store in the world. It was where,
in the early Nineties, as a music writer and reviewer, I
would hang out in the richly stocked classical music
annex, learning about new releases from knowledgeable

Tower staff, meeting with other writers, and attending the annual in-store appearances of opera stars like Luciano Pavarotti or Renée Fleming. Bin after bin of records, and later CDs, filled the aisles, while die-cut easel-backed posters of the new albums and beloved artists filled the empty spaces.

Rock-and-Roll Hall of Famer David Sholin, the man "with the golden ears" who changed the face of music programming on the radio, has similar memories of the San Francisco store:

> On Friday nights, the place was like an event. Just going in and seeing everybody in the place, the aisles jammed, all the new releases—it would be hard to describe to someone who wasn't there.[1]

But today, when I got to the corner of Columbus and Bay, the old beloved Tower—the Tower of Pavarotti and Fleming, U2 and the Rolling Stones, Madonna and Aretha—was dead. The windows of the old store were plastered with cheerless purple, red, and yellow signs bellowing the same out-of-tune song:

> *SALE ON EVERYTHING.*
> *NOTHING HELD BACK*
> *EVERYTHING MUST GO*
> *GOING OUT OF BUSINESS*

One week earlier, the fat lady had sung.

The price on the table was now $134.3 million. Cash.

The robust bidding had been going on for thirty hours. The once pristine law firm boardroom was littered with the debris of the marathon auction: ties and jackets of disheveled bidders sprawled on the backs of chairs, half-eaten pizza in soggy cardboard boxes, stacks of empty soda cans. But the end was finally in sight. After an auction lasting a full day and a half, all but two bidders had dropped out.

They called it a bankruptcy auction, but, in truth, it was the last picture show, the day when another piece of the music died. At 8:00 A.M. on Thursday, October 3, 2006, Tower Records, where we've been buying our music and our dreams for almost half a century, went under the hammer for the final time. Seventeen bidders had shown up at the offices of Delaware's largest law firm in downtown Wilmington to bid on the remains. And by 4:00 P.M. on Friday, October 4, only one liquidator and one low-end retailer were left standing.

It was the final stop on Tower's journey from a record department in a Sacramento drugstore, to America's best-known music retailer, to the latest victim of the digital revolution. Had there been any justice, the auction would have taken place on eBay, bringing an appropriately digital conclusion to the sad Tower story. The end had finally come for the store that had become synonymous with broad, deep choices in every musical genre—from jazz, country, classical, and opera to R&B, rap, and heavy metal.

The retailer had been in decline since the mid-Nineties, ever since the birth of the Internet. Big-box, low-cost retailers like Wal-Mart hadn't helped Tower's business. But the bigger culprit behind Tower's demise was the digital revolution. As a specialty retailer, it hadn't been able to compete against digital piracy or the low prices of Internet retailers like Amazon.com and iTunes.

Between 2003 and 2006, 800 independent music stores closed their doors for good. The independent record store is becoming an endangered species, especially in California, where a quarter of all music stores closed between 2003 and 2006. In the first five months of 2006 alone, 378 record stores closed nationally, against 106 closures in 2005. Ironically, the one record store that seems to be thriving today is the three-dimensional Sony BMG store on SecondLife.com, where virtual citizens seek to re-create the vitality of a real-life record store.

"We don't see the kids anymore," Thom Spennato, the owner of Sound Track, an independent record store in Brooklyn told the *New York Times* in July 2006.

That's because the kids are sitting at home in front of their computers, file-sharing digital music with one another—legally or illegally—or downloading 99-cent songs from iTunes.

The CD market plummeted 25 percent between 1995 and 2005. Between 1999 and 2005, music sales dropped by $2.3 billion from $14.6 billion to $12.3 billion. Global sales of music fell by another 4 percent in the first half of 2006, with revenues from physical formats such as compact discs down 10 percent.[2]

By the Friday afternoon of the Tower auction, the bidding for the chain was going up in $500,000 increments. The price on the table had risen to barely $130 million. It was a grim sum, given that Forbes had valued the company at $325 million in 1990. But sales, which had been in the $1-billion-a-year range during the Nineties, had dropped more than half since the digital revolution—bottoming out at $430 million in 2005.

The two parties left in the auction were the Great American Group, a California liquidator, and Trans World Entertainment, a New York low-end retailer, which had already rolled up the previously bankrupted Sam Goody and Wherehouse Music. They were bidding on everything: the entire inventory of CDs, DVDs, and books in the remaining eighty-nine stores in twenty states, as well as the Tower name.

Everything, that is, except Tower's 3,000 employees (including eighty-one-year-old founder Russ Soloman), the most valuable part of the company. None of the 3,000 flesh-and-blood people had any value to the liquidators at the Delaware auction.

At around 4:00 P.M. on Friday afternoon, Trans World Entertainment folded. Tower had been sold for $134.3 million. The Great American Group immediately announced their intention to liquidate. Tower Records was dead.

After a company barbecue in Sacramento, described

by participants as a funeral, Soloman wrote an emotional final e-mail to all his staff:

> The fat lady has sung. . . . She was way off key. Thank You. Thank You. Thank You.

At the Sunset Boulevard store, a marquee read, "It's the end of the world as we know it. Thanks for your loyalty." On the sidewalk, a mock gravestone was erected. It read, simply, "Tower." And at the flagship location in New York, Tower's row of blackened-out windows spanned the length of a city block that once thronged day and night with customers.

Inside the Bay and Columbus Street store, consumers were picking through the Tower carcass—the DVDs and CDs at 15 percent off, the books and magazines discounted by 30 percent. It was a miserable scene. I stood beside a shelf stacked with a reminder of music's glory days—compact discs of Pink Floyd's *Dark Side of the Moon* and the Beatles' *Abbey Road*. As people wandered past, I conducted my own on-the-spot research into Tower's demise.

"What will you miss?" I asked several shoppers.

"Choice," they replied. "Their deep, broad catalog. . . . Salespeople who love music. . . . Awesome selection. . . . Friday evenings and rainy Saturday afternoons browsing. . . . The serendipity of discovery of a new album or group. . . ."

The disappearance of Tower's unparalleled musical selection will certainly be mourned by all music lovers. As one Tower executive put it, "If you wanted the Amazon tree frog noises, we had it."

The expertise of the Tower staff will sorely be missed, too—the clerk who could have stepped out of Nick Hornsby's bestselling novel and film *High Fidelity*, the guy with the earring who has heard everything before anyone else, and who passes on that inside knowledge to the rest of the world. The people responsible for what Dave Marsh, the great rock critic, called "the transmission of music" from one generation to the next. This is no small thing. *Los Angeles Times* pop music critic Ann Powers confesses that a Seattle Tower clerk who turned her on to Elvis Costello and the Clash "changed my life."

Tower's remarkably diverse selection cannot be replicated. Perhaps no one summarizes the value of Tower's deep catalog better than Powers, who once worked as a clerk at the Tower on Bay and Columbus herself:

> Deep catalog was the commitment Tower made to the regular shopper: the jazzbo looking for that weird fusion project on the American Clavé label, the dreadlocked hippie browsing the Jamaican imports, the hard-core punk looking for anything with speedy guitars and a shouted chorus. By allowing its product buyers—a motley crew of aspiring musicians, bohemian lifers and undergrads willing to accept retail wages just to be near

all that music—to stock the shelves with virtually every pop derivative imaginable, Tower created a physical space where the music's variety came alive, where the snobbish geek and the casual listener were equally served.[3]

Ironically, Powers' "deep catalog" community sounds like a Silicon Valley vision of the digital future. Indeed, Chris Anderson's long tail of infinite musical choice could be a snapshot of the now defunct Tower store on Bay and Columbus.

But Tower's demise actually represents the end rather than the beginning of a long tail. By some estimates, Tower represented around 40 to 50 percent of the niche-genre labels' entire market. With Tower now closed, the niche labels have, in one fell swoop, lost half of their business. How these labels—in classical, jazz, opera, hip-hop, world, and the rest—are now going to reach the music-buying public is unknown. The sad truth is that with the demise of the physical record store, we may have less musical choice, fewer labels, and the emergence of an oligarchic digital retail economy dominated by Amazon.com, iTunes, and MySpace.

Chris Anderson, ever optimistic, would tell us that all the small labels can now sell directly, thereby no longer sacrificing their margins to middlemen. But doing so requires marketing skills and investment in Web site infrastructure and direct sales—specialized expertise that the majority of niche labels don't possess. A more likely consequence of Tower's closure is the increasing consolidation of the major labels—a development reflected by German media group Bertelsmann's choice to sell the publishing rights to the music owned by its BMG Music Publishing Group to Vivendi's Universal Music for $2.1 billion to raise cash for a buyout of one of their European partners.

Chris Anderson's *The Long Tail* claims that the future of music lies with the infinite selection of online stores like Amazon.com or iTunes. That may be true. But what these online stores don't have is the deeply knowledgeable Tower clerk to act as cultural tastemaker. Instead, our buying choices depend upon the anonymous Amazon.com reviewer—a very poor substitute for the bodily encounters that Tower once offered.

The Toy at the Bottom of the Cornflakes Box

One Saturday morning I found myself sitting opposite self-proclaimed music futurist Gerd Leonhard in San Francisco's Café Trieste. Leonhard is the author of *The Future of Music,*[4] a manifesto that imagines a world where music has become a public utility like water or electricity.

We couldn't have found a more appropriate spot to talk about the future of the recorded-music business. Located in the heart of the city's North Beach, a few blocks south of the now defunct Tower store on Bay and Columbus, this San Francisco landmark is a venerable

Italian café, lined floor to ceiling with black-and-white photographs of old opera divas. The Trieste is famous for its regular Saturday-afternoon concerts where local opera singers put on free shows for the café audience.

"Music will be a utility like water, like electricity, because essentially right now only two out of ten people are buying the music that they are listening to," the futurist shouted at me above the din. "But nine and a half out of ten are interested in music; together with sex and with games, it's the biggest thing on the Internet."

Leonhard's estimate of the number of people buying music was, in fact, far too optimistic. According to a joint 2006 report by European (IFPI) and American (RIAA) researchers, *forty songs* are actually downloaded for every legal music download. That adds up to 20 billion songs illegally downloaded in 2005, compared to a legal digital market of 500 million tracks, resulting in a paltry $1.1 billion in revenue.

Imagine the impact on the Café Trieste's bottom line if only one in forty coffee drinkers paid for their cappuccinos. But this is the reality of the digital economy. It's why the recorded-music industry doesn't have much of a financial future.

At the iTunes price of 99 cents a song, the 20 billion digital songs stolen in a single year adds up to an annual bill of $19.99 billion, one and half times more than the entire $12.27 billion revenue of the U.S. sound recording industry in 2005. That's $19.99 billion stolen annually from artists, labels, distributors, and record stores. Year by year, the entire music industry, which has brought us classic recordings of everyone from the Beatles, Pink Floyd, and The Clash to Luciano Pavarotti and Maria Callas, is being strangled by one of the most brazen mass larcenies in history.

"Just look around you," Gerd Leonhard told me, sweeping his hand across the crowded, noisy café. "Music has never been so popular."

The audience in Café Trieste indeed seemed captivated by the performance of the café's divas. The problem is, nobody was actually paying for it. The only money changing hands was in the sale of cappuccinos, pastries, and soda. It was not so dissimilar to what was happening on a far more vast scale on the Internet—art and culture being reduced to vehicles for the sale of other products.

Is this the future of music? As a free "come-on" to sell other stuff? Rather than a utility like electricity or water, music in the Web 2.0 revolution may become equivalent to the plastic toy found at the bottom of the cornflakes box.

Digital piracy and illegal file-sharing from services like BitTorrent, eDonkey, DirectConnect, Gnutella, LimeWire, and SoulSeek have become the central economic reality in the record business. It is why there are now 25 percent fewer music stores in America than there were in 2003. It is why the International Federation of the Phonographic Industry filed 8,000 new lawsuits against illegal downloaders in October 2006 alone. It is why, in the first half of 2006, shipments of CDs and other physical music formats in America were down 15.7 percent from the first half of 2005.[5] It is why there is no longer a "cultural hub" on the corner of San Francisco's Bay and Columbus Streets.

"If you can't beat 'em, join 'em" seems to have become the mantra of the increasingly desperate record industry. The situation has become so dire that labels are now planting decoys or fake files that contain messages from advertisers on peer-to-peer sites. For example, the rapper Jay-Z formed a 2006 alliance with Coca-Cola in which the Universal Music Group artist agreed to allow distribution of a clip from a live Radio City Music Hall performance on peer-to-peer sites. This clip came with a promotion for Coca-Cola and, thus, became a way for the soft-drink company to market their message to music thieves. Many other popular contemporary bands, including Audioslave, Ice Cube, and Yellowcard, are also selling advertising off the back of piracy.

"The concept here is making the peer-to-peer networks work for us," Jay-Z's attorney explained of this surreal strategy. "While peer-to-peer users are stealing the intellectual property, they are also the active music audience."

Given that only one in forty digital songs are being paid for, digital music is, like it or not, essentially free. For 98 percent of today's "consumers," music *is* now freer than electricity or water. And the recorded-music business is being forced to confront this *de facto* economic catastrophe head-on. Universal Music, the largest of the major labels, with millions of songs from artists as diverse as Eminem and Hank Williams, announced in September 2006 that it intended to freely distribute its catalogue on the Internet through a Web 2.0 service named SpiralFrog. A month earlier, EMI, another of the big four labels, announced a similar deal with a Web 2.0 company called QTrax. Both services give out the music for free on the Internet in exchange for exposing the listener to advertising.

To gain access to *Abbey Road* or *Dark Side of the Moon* on QTrax, will I have to first listen to a pitch for Q-Tips? Will future generations of opera fans who want to hear Mozart's opera *Così Fan Tutte* on SpiralFrog be interrupted at key moments by interstitials from the Italian airline Alitalia enticing them to visit Italy?

As Gerry Kearby, the founder and CEO of Liquid Audio, Silicon Valley's original digital music company, stated recently, "Perhaps the music is free, but inside the music is a condom or whatever the hell they are trying to sell you."

Services like QTrax and SpiralFrog threaten to reduce the experience of listening to music into a cat-and-mouse game between consumer and advertiser. And while Universal and EMI bring in money from Johnson & Johnson or Alitalia, the artists might get nothing in royalties.

Does the recorded-music industry have any alternative to partnering with services like SpiralFrog and QTrax? According to Web 2.0 idealists like Chris Anderson, the Internet offers musicians their own sales and marketing platform. But this doesn't translate into revenue. MySpace is now offering itself as a digital storefront by selling the music of three million unsigned bands. But as David Card, an analyst at Jupiter Research, said, "I've yet to see an entertainment company that can be successful by creating a business only out of the long tail."[6]

The problem is that even strong Internet visibility and popularity don't necessarily generate money. Take, for example, the band The Scene Aesthetic, a rock acoustic duo started by vocalist Eric Bowley and Andrew de Torres, a couple of twenty-year-old kids from Everett, Washington. Possessing the boyish good looks and gentle, self-conscious lyricism of a young Paul Simon and Art Garfunkel, The Scene Aesthetic have become huge stars on MySpace, YouTube, and PureVolume.com.

As of September 2006, the band, which posted its first song "Beauty on the Breakdown" on MySpace in January 2005, had built up nine million total plays on the social network, 2.3 million visitors had visited The Scene Aesthetic page on MySpace, and the duo had amassed more than 140,000 friends. On PureVolume.com, a free music site, its most popular album, *Building Homes from What We've Known,* had been downloaded 1.3 million times. On YouTube, the band's video of "Beauty in the Breakdown" had been watched half a million times.

And the total dollar revenue derived in digital music sales from its nine million plays on MySpace, the 1.3 million downloads on PureVolume.com, and the half million screenings on YouTube? Yes, you've guessed it. Zero.

In spite of their phenomenal online popularity, The Scene Aesthetic has yet to sign a record deal with a label. True, Eric Bowley was able to cobble together enough cash to quit his job selling televisions at Everett's Best Buy store and go on "national" tour in the summer of 2006. But the only gigs the band's amateur booking agent could leverage from their MySpace popularity were at such venues as the Wilton Teen Center in Connecticut, Todino's Pizza in Bloomington, Illinois, and Blue Ridge High School in Pinetop, Arizona. These venues, which seat about 200 fans and charge just $5 or $10 a head, barely cover the bands' hotel and travel costs. On good days, if the band manages to sell enough T-shirts and tickets, they can even buy dinner. On bad nights, Bowley and de Torres ended up sleeping on the basement floors of fans' homes.

This is no way for a band to become the next supergroup. Gerd Leonhard is right. Music is as popular now as it's ever been. But Internet fame doesn't equal dollars. The sheer volume of music online, and the ease with which it can be downloaded—for free—is snuffing out the careers of budding artists like The Scene Aesthetic. With so many songs available for free, or for 99 cents from iTunes and the like, why would anyone pay $15 to $20 for a CD? As a consumer, why buy an album when you can cherry-pick the one or two songs you really want? With fewer and fewer people buying the physical albums, where is the money for the record industry and the recording stars?

The Sound Aesthetic might still join the ranks of Arctic Monkeys and the handful of other bands who have managed to leverage their Internet popularity into commercial success. But their struggle to translate their massive virtual following into either significant record sales or a major label contract is an ominous augury for the other three million bands on MySpace trying to make a living selling their music.

The contrast between The Scene Aesthetic and Simon and Garfunkel is revealing. By the time Paul Simon and Art Garfunkel were Bowley's and de Torres' age, they already had a minor hit, "Hey Schoolgirl," which they recorded as the teenage duo Tom & Jerry and was released by Big Records in 1957. And by the time Simon and Garfunkel were twenty-three years old, they had their first album, *Wednesday Morning, 3 AM,* which was released on Columbia Records in October 1964 and contained their first hit song, "The Sound of Silence." That Bowley and de Torres will achieve comparable success in three years' time is unlikely.

In late October 2006, I had a conversation with Paul Simon about how the music business was being changed by the Web 2.0 revolution. Like Gerd Leonhard, Paul Simon confirmed that music today was as popular as it's ever been. But, unlike Leonhard, Simon wasn't optimistic about the future of high-quality recorded music.

To make a top-quality recording today, what he called an "exquisitely slow and detailed" album, Simon explained, ideally would take a full year and, given the price of top contemporary musicians, could cost a million dollars. But this kind of investment, he said, can't be earned back in a market where people are buying fewer and fewer compact discs. So recording artists necessarily compromise their music because it is not economically viable to hire the best musicians and take enough time making the recording.

"I'm personally against Web 2.0 in the same way as I'm personally against my own death," he said, in a line that might have been borrowed from one of his own songs.

But for all his antipathy, Simon is resigned to the Web 2.0 revolution, an event he compared to an uncontrollable forest fire. "Maybe," he said, "a fire is what's needed for a vigorous new growth, but that's the long view. In the short term, all that's apparent is the devastation." Citing what he called the "destruction" of the twentieth-century record business, he recalled the last verse from "Look at That," a song from his 2000 album *You're the One*. "You might learn something," Simon claims, one never knows. "But anyway, you've got to go."

But Simon wasn't finished. "We're going to 2.0," he concluded. "Like it or not, that is what is going to happen."

Perhaps Paul Simon is right. We're going to 2.0.

Like it or not.

5

the day the music died
[side b]

By the time Charles Dickens came to North America on a reading tour in 1842, hundreds of thousands of copies of his books—including *Sketches by Boz*, *Nicholas Nickleby*, *The Pickwick Papers*, and *Oliver Twist*—had been published in the United States. But Dickens "never derive(d) sixpence,"[1] because at the time, there was no copyright protection for works created in Britain and sold in the United States (and vice versa); U.S. publishers could copy British books without paying a dime in royalties.

Dickens and other authors with followings on opposite sides of the Atlantic—Henry Wadsworth Longfellow, Sir Walter Scott, and Harriet Beecher Stowe—were the early victims of intellectual piracy. By the 1840s, though a household name, Dickens was facing debtor's prison. Sir Walter Scott nearly went bankrupt in the middle of his career, and is said to have died at age sixty-one, "broken in body and mind by years of financial difficulties." And Harriet Beecher Stowe, an American, was estimated to have lost $200,000 (millions in today's currency) rightfully due her for European sales of *Uncle Tom's Cabin.*[2]

But, of course, had Dickens' rich character portraits or Longfellow's evocative poems never reached the opposite shores, the greater victims of piracy would have been readers. In any profession, when there is no monetary incentive or reward, creative work stalls. As Dickens, one of the first to actively lobby Congress for copyright protection, aptly noted, American literature could only flourish if American publishers were compelled by law to pay writers their due; allowing publishers to print the works of foreign authors for free would only discourage literary production.

Yet on the Web 2.0 such indiscriminate piracy is becoming the norm. "Booksellers, defend your lonely forts!" John Updike roused the book-loving audience at Book Expo America in late May 2006. Seventy-four-year-old Updike was in a feisty mood that day, shouting with the force and vigor of a man half his age. The object of his rage was Kevin Kelly, the "senior maverick" at *Wired* magazine who, earlier that month, had published his manifesto in the *New York Times Magazine* in support of the "universal book."

Kevin Kelly claims that the technology to digitize and

infinitely copy texts will inevitably overthrow hundreds of years of copyright protection. According to Kelly, we can no longer protect intellectual property from piracy, so all texts should be available for free. It is a bit like saying that because our car *might* get stolen, we should leave it unlocked with the keys in the ignition and the driver's-side door open, to usher would-be thieves on their way.

In Kelly's view (who, it doesn't hurt to note, has published several books for which he has received substantial advances), the value of the book lies not in the professional author's achievement in creating something true out of empty air and a blank page, but in the myriad ways the cult of the amateur can recall, annotate, tag, link, "personalize, edit, authenticate, display, mark, transfer and engage a work." According to Kelly, "The real magic will come . . . as each page in each book is cross-linked, clustered, cited, extracted, indexed, analyzed, annotated, remixed, reassembled, and woven deeper into the culture than ever before." In other words, a finished masterpiece like F. Scott Fitzgerald's *The Great Gatsby* is not important—what is important in today's digital world are the ways we annotate, link, and change to adapt the original texts. Fitzgerald's masterpiece is just a jumping-off point for what truly matters: the ways each of us annotate and remix, tag, and make it our own work. Fitzgerald was merely a skilled workman. To Kelly the real value of a work like *The Great Gatsby* is in what we—the amateur—bring to it.

Kelly argues that in the future, instead of making money on the sale of books, authors can "sell performances, access to the creator, personalization, add-on information, sponsorship, periodic subscriptions—in short, all the many values that cannot be copied." It's the old razor blade business model. The book is but a giveaway, and the writer will supposedly make money from consulting gigs, book signings, and public lectures.

But books aren't razors, and reading has nothing in common with shaving. As Updike shouted from the podium, "For some of us, books are intrinsic to our human identity." When writers, and composers and music makers for that matter, can no longer hope to make a living from their work, how many works will never be written or created? When there are no books to base talks on, no performances to sell merchandise at, no creators to greet and meet, and no music to sell ads with, culture and the industries that have arisen around it will wither and die.

Even Kelly admits that the protection of the physical copy has "enabled millions of people to earn a living directly from the sale of their art to the audience" and that it has "produced the greatest flowering of human achievement the world has ever seen." Isn't this a model worth preserving?

Hollywood in Crisis

But the economic consequences of the Web 2.0 revolution go far beyond just books and music. Thanks to pirated products, free news on the blogs, free radio from podcasters, and free digital classifieds on Craigslist, our media industries and content providers of all sorts—radio, television, newspaper, the movie businesses—are in decline. As *Atlantic Monthly* writer Marshall Poe told me, companies simply can't make money by providing high-quality content—be it music, movies, or news—for free. "The Internet is a huge moral hazard for people in general," he said, "and it is a huge economic hazard for the serious providers of content."

In the movie business, digital piracy, the explosion of free movie downloads, and the growing popularity of amateur video sites like YouTube and Veoh video are already causing a decline in box-office revenue and DVD sales.

Peter Jackson, the movie maestro who brought us the *Lord of the Rings* trilogy and the remake of *King Kong*, summed up the crisis succinctly: "Piracy has the very real potential of tipping movies into becoming an unprofitable industry, especially big-event films," he told the *International Herald Tribune* in August 2005.

Jackson's tipping point may have already arrived. In May 2006, LEK Consulting authored a report for the Motion Picture Association of America (MPAA), showing that the American movie industry lost $6.1 billion in global wholesale revenue to all forms of digital piracy in 2005; for the global movie industry, the figure was $18.2 billion. The LEK report, which was conducted over eighteen months and surveyed 20,600 movie consumers in twenty-two countries, showed that $2.3 billion of the losses stemmed from Internet piracy, $2.4 billion from street sales of bootlegged copies of DVDs and video cassettes, and the remaining $1.4 billion from the illegal copying of films in movie theaters. The MPAA's last official global revenue figures were of $44.8 billion in 2004.[3] In other words, piracy shaves around 12 to 13 percent off America's total movie industry revenue.

Another research group, the Texas-based Institute for Policy Innovation, argues that motion picture piracy results in a "total lost output" from all U.S. industries of $20.5 billion annually. Yes, that's right—$20.5 billion, including lost annual earnings to U.S. workers, lost tax revenue, and the loss of jobs across the economy.

According to MPAA's most recent statistics, the American movie business is in big trouble. In 2005, box office revenue was down 5.7% to $8.99 billion, and admission in movie theaters dropped 8.7 percent. In fact, admissions have dropped to their lowest levels since 1997. Most worrying of all, DVD sales, which had driven Hollywood studios' strong growth over the last decade, have now reached a plateau. This is due to the growing popularity of movie-downloading services (Wal-Mart, once one of the nation's leading DVD retailers, recently announced plans to offer one such service on its Web site). Pali Research analyst Richard Greenfield has forecast that 2007 will be the first year that DVD sales will decline in the United States.[4]

Nor has the Internet been the marketing solution to its economic crisis that the movie industry briefly hoped. New Line Cinema's 2006 horror movie Snakes on a

Plane was enormously hyped on the Internet and was expected, as a result, to be a big hit. New Line included ideas from bloggers in the script. They developed a Web site that allowed Internet users to receive telephone calls from the movie's star, Samuel L. Jackson. And they allowed anyone who purchased movie tickets online to participate in exit polls by sending text messages to the studio. But none of this buzz made any difference to the movie's bottom line. As the president of theatrical for New Line conceded to the *New York Times*, "There were a lot of inflated expectations on this picture. But it basically performed like a normal horror movie."[5]

Fewer people are paying to watch fewer movies in fewer theaters, and Hollywood is clearly feeling the pain. At the Walt Disney Company, domestic ticket sales plummeted from $1.5 billion to $962 million between 2003 and 2005, and studio entertainment revenues dropped 13 percent in 2005, largely due to lagging DVD sales. Recently, Disney was forced to eliminate 650 jobs and substantially cut the number of films it produces each year.[6] Disney isn't the only one downsizing. Paramount Studios also cut hundreds of jobs in their movie and DVD units, and Warner Bros. axed 400 jobs globally in December 2005, including its heads of comedy, casting, and scheduling.

But the worst is still to come. As the bandwidth revolution makes it increasingly easy to download movies from the Internet, Hollywood is about to become engulfed in the same storm that has wrecked the music industry. Today, according to research firm Park Associates, only 660,000 people regularly download movies from the Internet. Park expects this number to grow to 50 million by 2010.[7] Given the metrics on music thieves, 49 million of those downloaders are likely to be stealing.

The Internet is beginning to undermine the viability of the movie theater. ClickStar, an Intel-funded start-up founded by actor Morgan Freeman and launched in December 2006, is debuting some independent films on the Internet the same day they are released in the theaters. Such practices, which go against long-held Hollywood strategy, will compound the crisis facing movie theaters. When a movie is available on the Internet as soon as it has been released, why go to the extra inconvenience and cost of seeing it in a local theater? For many technophiles accustomed to watching all media on their computers already, the big screen viewing experience of the multiplex will hardly be missed.

It's not just movie theaters that are being undermined by the digital revolution. Local video stores are also under attack, thanks not only to piracy but also to the wildly successful Web-based operation Netflix. Video chains like Blockbuster are already hedging their bets by planning downloading services of their own in the future. But for local places, like Berkeley's Reel Video, an independent rental store stocking several thousand DVDs and videocassettes, the future is bleak.

"We'll always have a place," the *San Francisco Chronicle* quoted a clerk at Reel Video in October 2006. "We have a lot of obscure movies that you can't find any-where else."

Sure. Just as the Tower at Bay and Columbus had a lot of obscure music. Or the recently closed Cody's bookstore on Berkeley's Telegraph Avenue had a vast array of books.

Sadly, Cody's isn't alone. There's Duttons in Beverly Hills, A Clean Well-Lighted Place for Books in San Francisco, Coliseum Books, Enticott Books, and Murder Ink in Manhattan, and thousands of other beloved bookstores across America that have been forced to close their doors because of cut-priced e-competition from the Internet. According to numbers put together by the *New York Times*,[8] 2,500 independent bookstores have gone out of business since 1990. Meanwhile, Amazon.com, the online megastore and chief slayer of the independent bookstore, announced a 21 percent increase in "media sales" (which includes books) over the final quarter in 2005.

So what does Chris Anderson, the supposed champion of the little guy at the end of the Long Tail, think about all these closures? "The clear lesson of the Long Tail is that more choice is better," Anderson told the *Los Angeles Times* in February 2007. "Since bookstores can't compete on choice, many once-cherished stores are going to be road kill."[9]

But does the closure of independent stores result in more choice for consumers? Instead of 2,500 independent bookstores, with their knowledgeable, book-loving staffers, specialty sections, and relationships with local writers, we now have an oligarchy of online megastores employing soulless algorithms that use our previous purchases and the purchases of others to tell us what we want to buy. Like the death of Tower Records, the demise of the independent American bookstore means even less choice for the consumer—especially the book buyer who relies on their local bookstore for suggestions about interesting books.

Television stations, too, are navigating rough waters. More people are using DVR or TiVo, downloading shows through software like Azureus and Torrent, or getting their news online. As a result, fewer people are watching the commercials on both national and local stations that underwrite television, and advertisers are shifting more of their dollars online.

In historical terms, local television stations have represented what the *Wall Street Journal* called the "backbone" of the broadcast-TV business. But according to the Television Bureau of Advertising, total local broadcast revenue fell 9 percent in 2005 to $16.8 billion. The reason? Key sponsors like Daimler-Chrysler and Ford are cutting advertising budgets—13 percent and 15 percent, respectively—or moving online. With local stations failing to generate enough profits, corporate owners like Viacom, News Corp., and NBC Universal are selling them off. Some companies, like the Tribune Company, are even considering spinning off entire TV-station groups.

There was a time, not so long ago, when, if we wanted to watch television, we'd turn on our television sets. Now, we turn on our computers, flip open our cell phones, switch on our TiVos, or plug into our video iPods. The consequence of all this is perhaps best evidenced by the story that ran on the front page of several major papers on October 19, 2006: NBC Universal was slashing costs in news and prime-time programming. After three years of declining revenue, NBC Universal announced aggressive plans to save $750 million in operating costs and return the station to double-digit growth. The initiative, disturbingly dubbed "NBCU 2.0," included plans to eliminate 700 jobs, 5 percent of the company's total workforce. The first major TV company to acknowledge the limited growth potential of the television news business, NBC announced that most of its initial layoffs would be in the company's eleven news divisions; the company planned to cut spending on news programming and consolidate a number of local news stations. Former NBC correspondent David Hazinski predicted, "This trend will mean more processing, more in-studio things, probably more star celebrities to get people to watch based on the personalities, and less real news." According to a 2006 Pew Research study, 71 percent of adults in the key eighteen to twenty-nine age demographic already get most of their news online, where, as we have seen, information is often unreliable or biased. As television stations cut their news programming, this number will only increase.

When media companies flounder, employees and executives lose their jobs and shareholders lose their investments. But all the rest of us lose out, too, as the quality of programming is compromised. Case in point? NBC Universal also announced that its 8 to 9 P.M. time slot would no longer run high-cost, scripted dramas. Instead, this prime-time hour—one that has, over the years, featured favorites like *Friends* and *Seinfeld*, will now air cheaper-to-produce programming like the game show *Deal or No Deal* or more dime-a-dozen reality programs. According to Jeff Zucker, chief executive of NBC Universal's television group, "Advertiser interest just wasn't high enough to justify spending on scripted shows."

As they announced a $750 million cut in news programming and scripted dramas, NBC Universal also stated plans to invest $150 million in new digital projects and Internet offerings such as specialized broadband sites, actors' blogs, and Internet-only "webisodes," which are cheaper to produce and use unknown actors rather than the actual stars (like in the online version of *The Office*, in which Steve Carell is noticeably absent). As NBC Universal chairman Bob Wright told the *Wall Street Journal*, "As we reprioritize ourselves towards digital, we've got to be as efficient in our current businesses as possible. We can't have new digital expenses and the same analog expenses."

So, instead of the newest drama from Dick Wolfe or Aaron Sorkin, all we'll soon have to watch will be the Paris Hilton Channel, cheap knockoffs of existing sitcoms, reality television, or clips from Sam Waterston's video blog.

Radio is in the midst of its own identity crisis. Teenagers, historically radio's biggest and most devoted audience, simply aren't listening to radio anymore. Over the last ten years, the listening hours of eighteen to twenty-four-year-olds have dropped 21 percent. Since 2006, the stocks of the five largest publicly traded radio companies dropped between 30 percent and 60 percent. In the first six months of 2006 alone, the operating income of CBS' radio business declined 17 percent, forcing CBS to sell off some of its local radio channels. In the summer of 2006, The Walt Disney Company got out of the radio business entirely. And, in November 2006, Clear Channel, the largest radio operation in America, announced that it would be seeking offers for 448 of its 1,200 stations.[10]

When the Ink Bleeds Red

Traditional newspapers and magazines, too, are getting hammered by the free content and advertising on the Internet. Newspapers are getting smaller—in circulation, in ad revenue, and in relevance. They are even shrinking in physical size. The *Wall Street Journal* trimmed its width three inches in January 2007, reducing the space devoted to news by 10 percent and eliminating an entire column on the front page. The *New York Times* plans to trim its width by 1.5 inches,[11] as was done at the *Los Angeles Times,* where editors have also begun to push reporters for shorter stories, to cater to the attention span of the average online reader.

Circulation at America's newspapers is plunging. In the six months between March and September 2006, daily circulation for 770 newspapers in America was down 2.8 percent from the same period in the previous year—one of the worst declines on record.[12] The circulation of the *San Francisco Chronicle*, which lost $40 million just in 2004, fell over 16 percent between 2005 and 2006. The *Los Angeles Times'* circulation dropped 8 percent between 2004 and 2006; it has plummeted from its peak of 1.2 million in 1990 to its current circulation of 908,000—less than it was in 1968. The circulation of the Sunday edition of the *Boston Globe* dropped 25 percent between 2003 and 2006. The *Dallas Morning News'* circulation was down 13 percent in the first six months of 2006.[13] Even at the *New York Times*, where circulation remains relatively stable, predictions for the future are not optimistic; its share price has fallen 50 percent in the past 5 years.[14]

As circulations continue to drop, advertisers are shifting their dollars to online media, where they can reach a larger and more targeted audience. According to Merrill Lynch, in 2006 advertising sales at newspapers were flat and are predicted to drop in 2007—the first time in history that newspaper advertising revenue will have declined in a nonrecessionary year. The story is depressingly similar at almost every metropolitan and national newspaper. Advertising revenue at the *Boston Globe* was 12.4 percent less in the second quarter of 2006 than it was in the equivalent 2005 quarter. The *Wall Street Jour-*

nal's advertising revenue in September 2006 fell 5.9 percent compared to September 2005. The Belo Corporation, which publishes the *Dallas Morning News* and the *Providence Journal,* reported a 19 percent drop in general advertising revenue in the third quarter of 2006.[15] The migration of classified ads from print papers to free Web sites like Craigslist is draining even more revenue from newspapers. According to a report by the Pew Internet and American Life Project, the number of people who use online classified advertising through these services increased 80 percent in 2005, with almost nine million of those visitors using the free service on Craigslist.[16]

The first response to sagging revenue, of course, is layoffs. Predictably, the number of people employed in the industry, according to the Newspaper Association of America, fell by 18 percent between 1990 and 2004, largely due to downsizing and layoffs.[17]

More recently, The New York Times Company laid off 200 people in May 2005, including 130 at the *New York Times* itself and the rest at the *Boston Globe* and the *Worcester Telegram & Gazette.* Later that same year, another 500 jobs, or about 4 percent of the company's total workforce, were eliminated. The year 2006 was the annus horribilis for American journalists, with job losses surging 88 percent (from 9,453 job cuts in 2005 to 17,809 in 2006), according to the tracking firm Challenger, Gray, and Christmas.[18] In March 2006, the *Washington Post* announced plans to cut about eighty jobs from its newsroom over the next year. October 2006 was a particularly bloody month, with redundancy announcements from the *Plain Dealer* in Cleveland (sixty-five layoffs), the *San Jose Mercury News* (101 layoffs), the *Philadelphia Inquirer,* and the *Philadelphia Daily News.*

And in the fall of 2006, in a dramatic showdown that played out for months, Jeffrey M. Johnson and Dean Baquet, the publisher and editor of the *Los Angeles Times,* were very publicly ousted for refusing to carry out the budget cuts and firings ordered by the *Times'* parent company, the *Chicago Tribune.* Loyal employees of the company for a combined total of over twenty-five years, Johnson and Baquet had already complied with orders to cut 200 positions, or 20 percent of the newsroom employees, since the *Tribune* bought the paper in 2000. But when more cuts were ordered, they said enough was enough. Newspaper editors, Baquet declared in a fiery speech in New Orleans that precipitated his firing, must push back against cutbacks ordered by corporate owners in order to maintain the journalistic integrity and credibility of their papers.[19] Ironically, one important reason for the *Los Angeles Times'* financial crisis has been what the *Financial Times* called the "dramatic pullback" in Hollywood's spending on advertising (down 17 percent in 2006). It's the reverse of the new media ideal of synergy. Bad economic news in one sector of traditional media causes more bad news in another sector.

Things have not been much better in the magazine world. Time Inc. cut over 100 jobs in December 2005; in January 2007, they cut 300 more at popular magazines such as *People, Sports Illustrated,* and their flagship, *Time,* shutting down bureaus in Los Angeles, Chicago, Atlanta, Miami, and Austin. In August 2004, Gruner & Jahr USA, the publisher of major magazines such as *Fast Company, Fitness,* and *Family Circle,* announced plans to cut costs by $25 million and reduce staff by as much as 15 percent, before finally selling off the magazines entirely and taking a huge write-off.[20]

Those are a lot of lost jobs. Some will argue that seismic economic change always results in downsizing in one sector but the creation of jobs in another. The problem is, the Web 2.0 economy is not creating jobs to replace those it destroys. Take Craigslist, for example, which has done more to undermine classified newspaper advertising than any other single institution. In spite of being the seventh-most-popular Web site in the world, Craigslist operates out of a rickety Victorian building in a residential San Francisco district close to the Pacific Ocean and has an employee roster of twenty-two full-timers—the number of players on the field in a soccer game. But while these listings on Craigslist, a site founded in 1995 by a counterculturist named Craig Newmark whom *New York* magazine described as a "shlumpy IBM refugee,"[21] are ostensibly free, in reality they aren't. Every supposedly "free" new car or house or job advertisement takes money straight from a local newspaper. Bob Cauthorn, former VP of digital media at the *San Francisco Chronicle,* has estimated that Craigslist siphons off an annual $50 million from Bay Area newspapers alone. In other words, the people at the *Chronicle* and at the *San Jose Mercury News* who lost their jobs in 2006 can thank shlumpy Craig and his twenty-two employees and their "free" advertising.

Wikipedia, which is almost single-handedly killing the traditional information business, has only a small handful of full-timers, in addition to Jimmy Wales. It brings to mind Sir Thomas More's much-quoted remark from his 1515 satire *Utopia,* where, in reaction to the Enclosure Laws that banned the peasantry from the fields of the great estates, he wrote that "sheep are devouring men." Five hundred years later, in the Web 2.0 world, computers are consuming journalists with the same results: Many people are losing their livelihood, and a few lucky souls—landowning aristocrats in More's day and executives at companies like MySpace, YouTube, and Google in our own—are getting very very rich.

The YouTube guys are getting particularly rich. On Wednesday, October 11, 2006—just five days after eighty-nine Tower Record stores were sold for $134.3 million in a Delaware law office—Chad Hurley and Steven Chen, the founders of YouTube, had lunch with Google co-founder Larry Page and CEO Eric Schmidt in a booth at a Denny's near YouTube's small office in Silicon Valley. At the end of the meal, the four men agreed that the unprofitable YouTube, with its staff of sixty engineers, would be acquired by Google for $1.65 billion—a lot of money for a company at which amateurs create all the content for free. Since YouTube doesn't need journalists, editors, producers, publicists, customer-service staff, or a back-office support staff, this $1.65 billion is virtually all upside.

Of course, the demise of newspapers cannot all be blamed on the Internet. The rise of cable news, too, has contributed to newspapers' waning profit margins. And many newspapers are cannibalizing themselves by migrating to the Web, where there is typically free, unfettered access to the content. The print version of the *New York Times* has only 2.7 million paid subscribers (1.1 million to the daily papers and 1.7 to the Sunday edition), while the free online version receives 40 million users a month. The problem is that while the print version generates annual revenues of $1.5 to $1.7 billion a year, the online version pulls in just $200 million.[22] If people continue to migrate to the online version, the *Times* may be forced to rein in its editorial department and compromise its renowned editorial content. It may need to lure a wider audience made up of younger, less-educated readers with fluff pieces on entertainment and lifestyle topics in place of hard-hitting reporting on international affairs and politics.

This is already happening at some major papers. At the *Los Angeles Times,* which won fifteen Pulitzer Prizes between 2000 and 2005, managers have responded to declining circulation and advertising (daily circulation in 2005 was down 18 percent, and full-run advertising was down 26 percent) by pressuring editors to increase coverage of Hollywood and celebrity gossip. In October

2006, the paper launched an initiative christened The Manhattan Project (in an apparent reference to the gravity of its mission) to generate fresh ideas for stories expected to re-energize the paper and attract a wider readership. Most of these changes will likely involve linking the content of the print paper more closely to the online edition, which covers less hard news and more local events and entertainment.[23]

But what happens if even these tactics fail, and print papers are unable to retain the readership they need to stay economically viable? *The Economist* predicts that over the next few decades, half the newspapers in the developed world may fold.[24] The business model of the *New York Times* is instrumental to understanding the grave challenges that digital media pose to established newspapers. According to New York media maven Michael Wolff, for the *Times* to replicate its newsprint revenue would require it to either increase its online audience to around 400 or 500 million readers or to compromise its editorial content by catering to the interests of its advertisers. As Wolff put it:

> The *Times* as we know it, as a pastiche of its paper self, can't succeed online (the whole idea that an old-time business can morph seamlessly into a huge, speculative entrepreneurial enterprise is a kind of quackery). At best, it might become a specialized Internet player, having to drastically cut its current $300 million news budget. What it might providen-

tially become, however, is About.com, a low-end, high-volume information producer, warehousing vast amounts of advertiser-targeted data, harnessing the amateurs and hobbyists and fetishists willing to produce for a pittance any amount of schlock to feed the page-view numbers—and already supplying 30 million of the *Times*'s 40 million unique users.[25]

Should mainstream newspapers and television fold, where will online news sites get their content? Where will the Matt Drudges and the instapundits get their information? How can they comment on the war in Iraq, or the 2008 election, if there is no organization with clout and sufficient resources to report on it? In the absence of traditional news, will the online sites be forced to abandon the effort to search out the truth altogether and simply make the facts up? Who will have the resources to investigate and report on the next Watergate scandal or to pay the wages of the 2.0 versions of Carl Bernstein and Bob Woodward? Or will this kind of quality reportage simply cease to exist? As a 2006 report from the Carnegie Corporation of New York put it, "As newspapers begin to fade, are the institutions that replace them "up to the task of sustaining the informed citizenry on which democracy depends?"[26]

Wolff claims that the idea of the end of the *New York Times* is a "God Is Dead" sort of statement for an old guard Manhattan intellectual like himself. It's "too big, too existential" an idea to contemplate, he says. But the *New York Times* is only one small part of the story. Our entire cultural economy is in dire straits. I fear we will live to see the bulk of our music coming from amateur garage bands, our movies and television from glorified YouTubes, and our news made up of hyperactive celebrity gossip, served up as mere dressing for advertising. Will investigative reporting go the way of the peasantry in Thomas More's sixteenth-century England? In our coming digital future, God may not be dead—but commerce and culture may well be.

Where Is the Money?

Throughout history, art and culture have helped to bridge generations, establish a rich heritage, and generate wealth. Today, the primary value of Web 2.0 companies is in advertising dollars, not in establishing a rich cultural legacy. Take Google, for example, the economic paragon of a truly successful Web 2.0 media company. With a market cap of approximately $150 billion, the Silicon Valley company took in $6.139 billion in revenue and $1.465 billion in profits in 2005. What is telling is the fact that unlike companies such as Time Warner or Disney, which create and produce movies, music, magazines, and television, Google is a parasite; it creates no content of its own. Its sole accomplishment is having figured out an algorithm that links preexisting content to other preexisting content on the Internet, and charging advertisers each time one of these links is clicked. In terms of value creation, there's nothing there apart from its links.

The core of Google's business, 99 percent of its revenue, lies in its sale of advertising. In fact, of the $16 billion spent on online advertising industrywide in 2006, $4 billion, a whopping 25 percent, is estimated to have gone to Google.[27] Indeed, Larry Page and Sergei Brin, the multi-billionaire founders of Google, are the true Web 2.0 plutocrats—they have figured out how to magically transform other people's free content into a multi-billion-dollar advertising machine.

Indeed, one can argue that the entire Web 2.0 economy is a magnified version of Google. Over $500 million in venture capital was invested in 2006 in Web 2.0 me-too social media businesses like Bebo, Zimbra, Facebook, Six Apart, and Xanga, which offer nothing but the distribution of free user-generated content. The new, new thing in Silicon Valley is the "Bring-your-own-content" business model, in which sites that provide their users with nothing more than the platform to express themselves, network, and link with one another, are worth millions or billions of dollars. This idea is being exploited in every market from travel (RealTravel), to virtual communities (Second Life), to events planning (Zvents, Eventful, and Upcoming), to blogs (Technorati), to classifieds (Edgieo), to audio content (Podshow), to pornography (Voyeurweb). Even, absurdity of absurdities, to e-mails (FWDitOn).

In the first Internet boom, "eyeballs" (the number of views per page) was the criterion for determining the value of a Web company. Now, the value is determined by the number of pages of user-generated content potentially available for advertising. With money being pumped into online advertising increasing at an astronomical rate (total spending on Internet ads increased 30 percent in 2005 and another 28 percent in 2006), YouTube, MySpace, and Facebook are potential gold mines. That is why, despite having negligible revenues today, YouTube was acquired for $1.65 billion, MySpace went to News Corp. for $580 million (cheap at today's price), and Facebook is rumored to be worth upward of $1 billion. While MySpace may not be making money yet (according to *Fortune* magazine, it lost money in 2005), RBC Capital's Jordan Rohan predicts it will be worth $15 billion within three years.

Think about it. Fifteen billion dollars for a site containing nothing but user-created profiles. If each added page on MySpace increases the company's value, what's next? How about a social-networking business that offers amateurs cash each time they post a comment or upload a photo?

Don't laugh. This is not a long way off from Panjea. com's commitment to share 50 percent of its advertising profits with users who contribute their music or photography. YouTube is also flirting with the same crazy idea of a revenue-share to reward user "creativity." In January 2007, at the World Economic Forum in Davos, Switzerland, YouTube founder Chad Hurley told the BBC that his company was working on a technology that would give users a share in the company's ad revenue.[28]

So while our record stores, newspaper companies, and

radio stations are struggling just to survive, we're pumping all our money instead into businesses that offer nothing more than infinite advertising space in exchange for user-generated nonsense that couldn't be published or distributed through any professional source.

God Is Dead

My own "God Is Dead" moment came in late 2005. I was talking with Alan Parsons, the legendary record producer best known for engineering the Beatles 1969 album *Abbey Road* and Pink Floyd's 1973 album *Dark Side of the Moon.*

Both albums are huge economic successes. As of 2004, sales of *Dark Side of the Moon* were at over forty million units, making it the twentieth-bestselling album in history. And *Abbey Road,* with its iconic cover photograph of the Beatles crossing a North London street, is the forty-sixth-bestselling album of all time, and has gone platinum fifteen times.

Abbey Road and *Dark Side of the Moon* represent the apotheosis of the mass media economy that shaped the twentieth century. These albums made mass cultural, political, and social statements that may never again be repeated. And they made money, too. In 2002, *Dark Side of the Moon* was still selling 400,000 copies, making it the 200th-bestselling album of the year, almost thirty years after its initial release.

I had first met Parsons at a Silicon Valley conference

called "Media Business Five" (MB5), which I produced in the fall of 2000. I invited a hundred leading media visionaries to imagine the future of the information and entertainment industries.

"Where is the money?" was the question I asked everyone at MB5.

In addition to Parsons, MB5 alumni included Jonathan Taplin, the Hollywood insider who produced Martin Scorcese's *Mean Streets;* Frank Casanova, head of Streaming Media at Apple; Chuck D of Public Enemy and the first serious rap artist; Chris Schroeder, then-CEO of the online *Washington Post;* Michael Robertson, founder of MP3.com; and many other leading figures in Silicon Valley and Hollywood.

When I spoke to Parsons in 2006, he announced the end of the record business as we know it. My original question at MB5—Where is the money?—still couldn't be answered. By 2005, Parsons had concluded it would *never* be answered. The record business was dying. The party had come to an end.

"Are you sad?" I asked him.

"It's very sad, yes," he said. "But I'm glad I've lived through the—what's the word—the glorious years."

There might be money to be made by linking music to advertisements, or other content to the sale of condoms or cappuccino. But the glory days of selling epoch-making albums like *Abbey Road* are over.

Today, the lyrics from a song like "Money" on *Dark Side of the Moon* reverberate with a strange irony. In a way they describe Parsons' "glorious years"—the dying gasps of mass media when an album sold forty million units in record stores like Tower, and thievery was limited to small-scale, in-store shoplifting rather than an industry-destroying, paradigm-shifting dismantling of 200 years of intellectual property law. As the biggest record store in the world closes its illustrious doors on the corner of Bay and Columbus, we say good-bye to one of the most venerated culture industries of modern times.

6

moral disorder

When Yours Is Mine

Thou Shalt Not Steal.

n the summer of 2003, twelve-year-old Brianna LaHara discovered the addictive pleasure of downloading online music. Instead of spending vacation days riding bikes with friends or lounging at the community pool, this New York City middle schooler sat at her computer and illegally downloaded over 1,000 songs before copying and distributing them among friends using file-sharing applications. She thought nothing of it until that September, when the Recording Industry Association of America knocked on her door, informing her that she was being named as a defendant in one of 261 lawsuits being filed in a crusade to crack down on "exclusively egregious file swappers." (The case was eventually settled out of court.)

Was LaHara running an international ring of digital thieves, or had she simply committed the naive mistake of an unwitting youth? Of course, she was no hardened felon—in fact, she had had no idea she was doing anything wrong. "I thought it was OK to download music because my mom paid a service fee for it," she told the *New York Post.* Technically, her paid subscription did not entitle her to download, copy, and share songs. But in an era where file sharing, music downloading, and cutting and pasting—especially among the younger set—is the norm, is what she did really that surprising? But as innocent as LaHara's intentions were, the fact remains that theft of intellectual property on today's Web 2.0 is as pervasive—and potentially as destructive—as a new strain of avian flu.

The Judeo-Christian ethic of respecting others' property that has been central to our society since the country's founding is being tossed into the delete file of our desktop computers. The pasting, remixing, mashing, borrowing, copying—the *stealing*—of intellectual property has become the single most pervasive activity on the Internet. And it is reshaping and distorting our values and our very culture. The breadth of today's mass kleptocracy is mind-boggling. I'm not referring only to the $20 billion pilfered and pickpocketed, day by day, from the music industry or the $2.3 billion and growing from the movie industry. Sadly, the illegal downloading of music and movies has become so commonplace, so ordinary, that even the most law-abiding among us, like Brianna LaHara, now do it without thinking. "How are we supposed to know it's illegal?" asks a bookkeeper in Redwood City, California, as he copied a playlist of songs to give out to his friends as a party favor.

The problem is not just pirated movies and music. It's become a broader quandary over who-owns-what in an age when anyone, with the click of a mouse, can cut and paste content and make it their own. Web 2.0 technology is confusing the very concept of ownership, creating a generation of plagiarists and copyright thieves with little respect for intellectual property. In addition to stealing music or movies, they are stealing articles, photographs, letters, research, videos, jingles, characters, and just about anything else that can be digitized and copied electronically. Our kids are downloading and using this stolen property to cheat their way through school and university, passing off the words and work of others as their own in papers, projects, and theses.

A June 2005 study by the Center for Academic Integrity (CAI) of 50,000 undergraduates revealed that 70 percent of college students admitted to engaging in some form of cheating; worse still, 77 percent of college students didn't think that Internet plagiarism was a "serious" issue. This disturbing finding gets at a grave problem in terms of Internet and culture: The digital revolution is creating a generation of cut-and-paste burglars who view all content on the Internet as common property.

This warped definition of intellectual property and ownership isn't confined to students and digerati alone.

These days, even the clergy are turning into plagiarists. With sites like sermoncentral.com, sermonspice.com, and desperatepreacher.com offering easily downloadable transcripts of sermons, more and more pastors, according to the *Wall Street Journal,* are delivering recycled sermons, almost verbatim, without crediting their original author. "There's no sense reinventing the wheel," says Florida pastor Brian Moon, who admits to delivering a sermon that he bought for $10 on another pastor's Web site. "If you got something that's a good product, why go out and beat your head against the wall and try to come up with it yourself?"[1] In our Web 2.0 world, it's just so easy to use other people's creative efforts; even our priests, whom we expect to be paragons of virtue, are doing it.

Stanford University law professor Lawrence Lessig argues that "legal sharing" and "reuse" of intellectual property is a social benefit. In fact, as I discussed in Chapter 1, Lessig wants to replace what he calls our "Read-Only" Internet with a "Read-Write" Internet, where we can "remix" and "mashup" all content indiscriminately. Lessig, misguided as he is, suggests that digital content—whether it be a song, a video, a short story, or a photograph—should be commonly owned for the benefit of everyone. What Lessig fails to acknowledge is that most of the content being shared—no matter how many times it has been linked, cross-linked, annotated, and copied—was composed or written by someone from the sweat of their creative brow and the disciplined use of their talent.

Of course, one can't blame digital technology alone for this explosion of plagiarism and illegal downloading. The Web 2.0 culture grew up celebrating file sharing; and now it has provided, on a mass scale, the tools that make cheating and stealing so much easier and so much more tempting. Addictive, almost. With the digital world at each of our fingertips, why not, and besides, who's to know? After all, as any shoplifter will tell you, it's a lot easier to steal if you don't have to look the shopkeeper in the eye.

The fact is that co-opting other people's creative work—from music file sharing, to downloading movies and videos, to passing off others' writing as one's own—is not only illegal, in most cases, but immoral. Yet the widespread acceptance of such behavior threatens to undermine a society that has been built upon hard work, innovation, and the intellectual achievement of our writers, scientists, artists, composers, musicians, journalists, pundits, and moviemakers.

Stanford University professor Denise Pope tries to explain away cheating as a consequence of the excessive academic pressures on kids. "On the part of students, there's an eerie logic to justify cheating. It's three o'clock in the morning, you're exhausted, you've worked hard. . . . Rather than getting a zero, you'd take your chances with plagiarism."[2]

But students who cheat aren't genuinely learning anything. And by depriving artists and writers of the royalties due them, they aren't just hurting those from whom they steal—in the end, they are hurting us all.

moral disorder

Betting the House

The nineteen-year-old bank robber held a handwritten note in his sweaty palms. The rush he experienced was like the feeling he had when he played poker online. The same mix of euphoria and nausea. The same rapid heartbeat, the same parched mouth, the sense that his face was on fire. The same feeling of powerlessness, as if he weren't the author of his own actions.

Then he slid the note across the counter toward the bank teller. It was as if somebody else had scrawled the message. As if somebody else were robbing the bank.

I WANT $10,000 IN CASH. I HAVE A GUN! BE QUIET AND QUICK, OR I WILL SHOOT. NO BAIT!

In his mind, everything went silent. It was the same silence that followed the final raise in an online poker game. In the sleepy little Pennsylvania bank, time stood still. Everything froze.

It was the teller's move. Would she fold and hand him the cash? Or would she call his bluff on the gun?

The Wachovia Bank teller, a local Allentown woman named Hiyam Chatih, stared at the baby-faced teenager standing in front of her. Dressed in a green fleece jacket and a red baseball cap, he resembled an altar boy gone off the rails. His glazed stare and disheveled state suggested drug addiction or demonic possession.

Chatih folded; emptying her till, she handed him

$2,871 in used banknotes. He stuffed them into his back-pack and ran out into the snowy afternoon. There, beside the shoveled walkway, the getaway car, a black Ford Explorer, waited for him. He jumped in, and the car roared off into the late-gathering gloom.

Later that evening, the robber was apprehended by armed police on the nearby campus of Lehigh University, when the young desperado, who also happened to be the second cellist in the Lehigh Philharmonic, showed up for nightly orchestra practice.

His name was Greg Hogan. In addition to being a member of the university's philharmonic orchestra, Hogan was the President of Lehigh's Class of 2008 and the assistant to the university chaplain.

"Mom, I'm in bad shape," the Lehigh sophomore confessed into a cell phone, after he'd been booked by the cops for bank robbery. "I've done something really stupid."[3]

Why did the President of the Class of 2008 wreck his life for $2,871? The reason was simple. Greg Hogan had become addicted to Internet gambling.

In the twelve months leading up to his bank heist, the Lehigh sophomore was down $7,500. He had forty-five bank overdrafts. He owed money to his parents, siblings, and Sigma Phi Epsilon fraternity brothers. He had emptied his own family's safe of $1,200 in bonds saved for him since his birth. What started as a $75 bet on pokerstars.com became a single-minded obsession. Hogan was soon skipping classes, missing meals, and going on sleepless binges that lasted fourteen hours at a time.

Soon, online poker had taken over his life. So it was fitting that the heist resembled the final hand in a game of high-stakes hold 'em. The last big raise, in this case, would result in ten years behind bars.

The son of an Ohio Baptist minister, Hogan was a musical prodigy who, by the age of thirteen, had twice given piano recitals at Carnegie Hall. He was home-schooled by his mother until the age of fourteen, when he won a scholarship to Ohio's exclusive University School. There, he excelled musically and academically, playing both cello and piano in the school orchestra and working as a Young Republican volunteer for leading Ohio politicians and judges. On graduation, Hogan selected a quote by Winston Churchill for his senior yearbook page: "History will be kind to me, for I intend to write it." At Lehigh, the gregarious Hogan did indeed write his own history, but not quite as he might have expected.

Hogan isn't alone in his secret addiction. Thanks to sites like PartyGaming, SportingBet, 888.com, BetonSports, and Bodog.com, Internet gambling has quickly became a national disease. In 2005, the year Hogan robbed the Allentown Wachovia Bank, $60 billion was bet on online poker alone. That year, according to Annenberg Public Policy Center research, an estimated 1.6 million college students and 1.2 million kids under twenty-two were gambling regularly online, and the number of male college students gambling online on a weekly basis quadrupled. Some college students are so addicted to online gambling that they are spending all their waking hours glued to their laptop screens, never leaving their broadband-enabled dorm rooms, sometimes even falling asleep in the middle of a hand.

Research scientists tell us that online gambling is as addictive as cocaine, alcohol, and other substance abuse. A 2006 study by Dr. Nancy Petry, an expert on online gambling at the University of Connecticut Health Center, says that over 65 percent of Internet gamblers are pathologically addicted, and that Internet gamblers are far more likely to be addicted to gambling behavior than those who frequent the real-world casinos. Why? Because unlike real casinos, which require you to travel to where they are located, these sites can be accessed from anywhere, twenty-four hours a day. According to Petry, "The availability of Internet gambling may draw individuals who seek out isolated and anonymous contexts for their gambling behaviors. Accessibility and use of Internet gambling opportunities are likely to increase with the explosive growth of the Internet."[4]

Internet poker is fast becoming the opium of the college crowd. With campuses so fully wired with broadband connections, addicts can place wagers from their dorm rooms, study lounges, even while sitting in class. As a result, cases like Hogan's are far from rare. "It fried my brain," confessed a kid from Florida who lost a quarter of a million dollars on online poker. "I would roll out of

moral disorder

bed, go to my computer, and stay there for twenty hours. One night after I went to sleep, my dad called. I woke up instantly, picked up the phone, and said, 'I raise.' "

In a June 2006 *New York Times Magazine* exposé on online gambling, Mattathias Schwartz blames the colleges for this national pandemic: "Administrators who would never consider letting Budweiser install taps in dorm rooms have made high-speed Internet access a standard amenity, putting every student with a credit card minutes away from twenty-four-hour, high-stakes gambling."

The growth of the online gambling sector recalls what happened when the European powers exported opium to China in the eighteenth century. It resulted in the same nightmarish consequences—powerless addicts, a pandemic of opium dens, a demoralized, destabilized population. By the end of the nineteenth century, over half of China's population were opium addicts, and Chinese society had become unraveled. Could this happen to us today, online? Could a growing segment of our population, like Greg Hogan, lose control of their lives?

One can see how seductively easy online gambling is. Just switch on your computer, type in a URL, and you're in virtual Las Vegas. Broadband delivers a twenty-four-hour, nonstop, personalized city of sin to every dorm room and every off-campus apartment in every college in America. It's the equivalent of Vegas on steroids.

In *Amusing Ourselves to Death*, his 1985 polemic against the trivialization of American life, Neil Postman argues that Las Vegas had become a "metaphor of our national character and aspiration, its symbol a thirty-foot-high cardboard picture of a slot machine and a chorus girl." Today, in the Web 2.0 epoch, Postman sounds as dated as Gibbons describing the decline of the Roman Empire. That poster of a slot machine has been digitalized and virtualized and is now ubiquitous and available at all times. Nobody needs to travel to Las Vegas—Las Vegas now comes to us. As Schwartz wrote about college students and Internet gambling:

> Freshmen arrive already schooled by ESPN in the legend of Chris Moneymaker, the dough-faced 27-year-old accountant who deposited $40 into his Pokerstars.com account and parlayed it into a $2.5 million win at the World Series of Poker in Las Vegas. Throughout the dorms and computer labs and the back rows of 100-level lecture halls, you can hear the crisp wsshhp, wsshhp, wsshhp of electronic hands being dealt as more than $2 billion in untaxed revenue is sucked into overseas accounts each year.

For a year, Greg Hogan had carried his Las Vegas around with him wherever he went. *Wsshhp, wsshhp, wsshhp.* He would sometimes play Texas Hold 'em for four days straight in his dorm room. In the computer lounges of the Lehigh library, he pulled all-nighters playing 60 to 100 hands an hour. He even brought his own casino to his clergyman father's basement office in Ohio during the winter vacation, where, with the music of Green Day, Incubus, and 311 blaring in the background, he celebrated Christmas by playing nonstop digital poker with other anonymous addicts around the world.

Like theft, gambling has existed long before the Internet, probably as far back as the beginnings of human civilization. But the proliferation of casinos and online gambling has dramatically heightened our addiction to gambling by reducing much of the social stigma and allowing us to gamble, surreptitiously or not, anywhere at any time: from our homes, our offices, on our commute to work, or even on the sidelines of our kids' soccer games.

Online gambling is prohibited in the United States under the 1961 Federal Wire Act. Yet, until the summer of 2006, not a single site had ever been indicted and the industry thrived, generating around $6 billion of revenue in America in 2005.[5] Businesses like BetonSports, 888.com, SportingBet, and PartyGaming grew up overnight, basing their computer servers offshore in tax-free Costa Rica, Gibraltar, Antigua, and the Channel Islands, where they were largely ignored by American law enforcement. Only now, as we shall see in Chapter 8, is the danger of online gambling being confronted.

A significant portion of society feels that adults are responsible for their own actions, that they should be free to gamble their lives away if they wish. But the social costs of the online gambling culture extend far beyond the destruction of individual lives. Families become unglued. Desperate addicts go to desperate and sometimes criminal lengths to get their hands on more cash. Any way you look at it, online gambling is dangerous and illegal, and by doing nothing to clamp down on it, the government undermines our faith in the rule of law.

Moreover, Internet gambling sends a terrible message to our kids about the value of money. The easy-come, easy-go attitude that online gambling instills is an insidious ethic to pass on to our kids. Online gambling feeds a kid's fantasy of getting something for nothing.

Greg Hogan was seduced by the promise of easy-money poker when he saw the $160,000 in winnings of another student gambler. To the naive eighteen-year-old, that kind of money could have been his if he played his cards right, if you'll excuse the pun. The irony is that if he had simply worked and studied hard throughout college, he could have ended up with a high-flying career on Wall Street or Main Street that would have ultimately been far more lucrative.

Most Silicon Valley pundits would, of course, snigger at the old-fashioned celebration of hard work, self-discipline, frugality, and self-sacrifice. Maybe that's because the Web 2.0's YouTube economy, with its irrational valuations and instant millionaires, where a couple of twenty-something kids can cash in $1.65 billion and over $300 million apiece in stocks for an unprofitable eighteen-month-old Internet site, has infiltrated and infected the rest of America with irrational attitudes and beliefs. Gambling—with its illusionary shortcut to instant wealth—has become a way of life not only in Silicon Valley but in society at large.

Perhaps we can't overcome online gambling any more than we can outlaw other addictive Internet obsessions, like pornography and file sharing. But don't we have a responsibility in society to try to control these behaviors so that they don't become the opium of the twenty-first century? As James Madison, one of America's wise founders, once remarked, we aren't angels. We don't always do the right thing. That is why we have enacted laws that help us regulate our darker impulses and behaviors.

Of course, this is first and foremost a moral issue, and the Web 2.0 world is uncomfortable with ethical debate. It raises questions about the kind of society we want and the kinds of kids that we seek to raise.

One thing is for sure—we don't want to raise a generation of Greg Hogans. So perhaps, just as alcohol needs to be restricted to licensed establishments that can check IDs and be held accountable if their patrons drink too much and attempt to drive, legal gambling needs to be confined to licensed casinos—rather than allowed inside dorm rooms and university libraries.

Sex Is Everywhere

The ways in which the Web 2.0 is compromising our morals and our values is most evident in the realm of pornography. Between 1998 and 2003, the *Internet*

Filter Review reported, the amount of Internet pornography mushroomed 1,800 percent from 14 million to 260 million pages.[6] The number of pornographic sites has multiplied, too—seventeenfold, in fact, from 88,000 porn sites in 2000 to 1.6 million in 2004.

Not surprisingly, addiction to online pornography has risen dramatically, as well. The National Council on Sex Addiction and Compulsivity believes somewhere between 3 percent and 8 percent of Americans are "sex addicts" in some shape or form, and the San Jose Marital and Sexuality Center estimates that between 6 percent and 15 percent of online pornography users are "compulsive," spending at least eleven hours a week on porn sites. As a consequence, twelve-step programs for pornography addiction are springing up all over America.

The Web 2.0 twist to this explosion of addictive smut is the rise in user-generated pornography. Amateur porn sites that subsist on user-generated content like Voyeurweb, or Pornotube, a rip-off of YouTube that posts thousands of new amateur pornographic videos weekly, are among the most highly trafficked sites on the Web. In fact, according to traffic-ranking authority Alexa.com, Pornotube—founded in February 2006—has, in just one year become one of the top two hundred most-popular Web sites, with significantly more daily visitors than "professionally" created porn sites like playboy.com.

More sobering, the National Center for Missing and Exploited Children (NMEC) estimates that the number of images of child porn on the Internet has increased by

1,500 percent. One would have to be in the pay of the ACLU not to see that this poses real concerns for both the future of an open Internet and for the moral tenor of our society. Yes, most civilized societies have their red-light districts and peep shows, and pornographic DVDs have been a high-growth industry for years. But it wasn't until the advent of the Internet, and the rise of amateur content on the Web 2.0, that porn has become so ubiquitous, so available, so diverse and perverse in its offerings that it is virtually inescapable.

This is no exaggeration. In a telephone survey of 1,500 Internet users between the ages of ten and seventeen, the Crimes against Children Research Center at the University of New Hampshire found that of the 42 percent of kids who were exposed to online pornography, 66 percent reported that this exposure was "unwanted." This report, released in January 2007, suggests that a shocking two-thirds of our kids who see online pornography are doing so against their will.[7] As Dr. Michael Wasserman, a pediatrician with the Ochsner Clinic in Metairie, Louisiana, put it, "It's beyond the Wild West out there."

To many parents of teenage and pre-teenage kids, including myself, hard-core online pornography is a moral scourge. Do you want your kids trawling around voyeur.com (where they could catch the amateur porn show of a neighbor or teacher)? What kind of lessons are they learning online about real love and the role of sex in a mature relationship? How can they *not* come away with a twisted notion of what sex is about? Is it okay that our kids are being exposed to this twisted content with every spam e-mail solicitation and pop-up advertisement?

Web 2.0's social-networking sites are certainly not helping to prevent pornography addiction among minors. On MySpace, fourteen-year-old girls, with screen names like "nastygirl," post photos in which they pose provocatively in their underwear, bathing suits the size of postage stamps, skin-tight leather clothing, or cleavage-revealing tops. This is the "culture" that the online cult of the amateur promotes and perpetuates. How far have things gone? In February 2006, *Playboy* magazine issued a casting call for a "Girls of MySpace" nude magazine spread.

And this is the tamer fare. Solicitations of sex among young teens and preteens on sites like MySpace are becoming commonplace. Message boards on MySpace have become confessionals on which thirteen- and four-teen-year-olds one-up each other with boasts about their sexual exploits and experimentations. While no one over the age of eighteen can access a fourteen- or fifteen-year old's profile without knowing their full name or e-mail address (unless, of course, they lie about their age, which people routinely do), fourteen- and fifteen-year-olds can view any profile they wish. Inevitably, they begin to mimic the offensive and lewd material posted by older members.

What's more, social-networking sites are reaching kids at younger and younger ages. The *Wall Street Journal* recently reported that in December 2006, 22 percent of all visitors to MySpace were under the age of eighteen.

And sites targeted at eight- to twelve-year-olds—such as clubpenguin.com, imbee.com, and tweenland.com—are springing up like mushrooms after a spring rain to mimic the popularity of MySpace. Some of these sites receive as many as two million visitors a month. While theoretically there are parental controls in place, they are easy to circumvent. Kids often use code words and acronyms to trick the content filters and use their parents' password to bypass controls and sign themselves in.

I would argue that the ubiquitous sex on the Internet and the hypersexual content of online social-networking sites is accelerating kids' sexual and social development in very dangerous ways. Need proof? The online sex magazine *Nerve* recently published an interview with a thirteen-year-old eighth-grade girl named "Z" about Internet pornography:[8]

> **NERVE:** *Have you ever seen any pornography on the internet?*
>
> **Z:** Obviously.
>
> **NERVE:** *How old were you would you estimate when you first saw porn?*
>
> **Z:** I guess ten, but that was because there were pop-ups, like advertisements, shit like that.
>
> **NERVE:** *So do you know anyone who's really into internet porn?*
>
> **Z:** Basically all of my friends are.
>
> **NERVE:** *Are you?*

z: Yeah. I'm not like ashamed to say that. Most of the time the way my friends look at it it's not like, "Oh my God, that's so hot." It's like, "Yeah, that's all right." I sort of like gothic porn.

Thirteen-year-olds should be playing soccer or riding bikes, not sitting in locked bedrooms looking at hard-core pornography. The Internet is transforming future generations into a nation of kids so inundated by and desensitized to hard-core smut that they've even developed genre favorites. And what the heck is *gothic porn?*

But, of course, this is hardly the darkest, scariest part of online sex. The fact is, social-networking sites have become magnets for real-life sexual predators. Thanks to the vast amount of detailed personal information kids post on their profiles—including hometown, school location, favorite hangouts, and, of course, photos— pedophiles have never had an easier time acquiring sexual images of underage kids or of tracking down their potential victims in the real world.

The dangers of a social-networking site like MySpace are horribly real. In January 2007, the families of four girls ages fourteen and fifteen sued MySpace for failing to provide safety measures for protecting their daughters from sexual predators, after the girls had been sexually abused by men whom they met on the MySpace Web site.[9] We all have a responsibility to protect our kids from a similarly premature end to their age of innocence.

Online Addiction

Forty-seven-year-old Carla Toebe couldn't control her Internet dating habit.

The first thing this mother of four would do in the morning, before getting out of bed, was boot up her laptop and begin chatting and instant messaging on online dating sites. Often, she would spend as many as fifteen hours on these sites, rarely leaving her bed and ignoring her daily tasks, leaving her Richland, Washington, home at times with stacks of unwashed dishes and dirty laundry. "I am self-employed and need the Internet for my work, but I am failing to accomplish my work, to take care of my home, to give attention to my children who have been complaining for months," she wrote.[10] She had become a slave to the digital universe, preferring her online existence to the day-to-day realities of life itself.

Internet addiction is not new. But in a Web 2.0 world in which so much of our lives—from social networking, to exchanging ideas, to watching videos, to self-broadcasting—is conducted online, Internet addiction is inevitably on the rise. According to a recent Stanford University study, Internet users are now averaging 3.5 hours a day online, and in the first scientifically rigorous research project, conducted by the Stanford University School of Medicine, on the addictive properties of the Internet, it was found that out of 2,513 adults, more than one in eight manifested some symptom of Internet addiction.

Beyond the disturbing individual stories of women like Carla Toebe, there are many other symptoms of this incipient social disease. As we have seen, addiction to online theft, gambling, and pornography has become a social curse afflicting everyone from twelve-year-old digital-music downloaders, to college-age poker players, and pornography-obsessed teenagers. Indeed, in the age of always-on media, Internet addiction is corrupting our values and culture.

Our Second Lives

The popularity of online multiplayer games like Second Life, where users create online personas and engage in any and every form of real-life activity—from starting a business, to getting married, to buying and decorating a home is resulting in dangerous confusion between virtual reality and life. Virtual worlds like Second Life, which has grown from 100,000 users at the end of 2005 to 1.5 million by the end of 2006, are becoming highly addictive alternatives to the pressures and frustrations of the real world. The addiction here is to a consequence-free existence, where absolutely anything—including being able to fly, becoming a different gender, even killing someone without real-world repercussions—is possible. And, for many, that is irresistibly seductive.

Second Life has a thriving virtual economy based on Linden dollars, which users can purchase with real money. On Second Life, real developers sell virtual land, real advertising executives sell virtual billboard space, real clothing retailers sell virtual clothing, real hotel chains sell virtual rooms, and real therapists sell virtual counseling sessions to real couples. In January 2005 alone, players spent over $5 million in transactions for virtual items.[11] While this makes the site a potentially lucrative source of income for entrepreneurial types, it can have dangerous financial consequences for addicts who prioritize their second lives over their real lives and drain their bank accounts buying goods and services to consume in their second lives.

And because, in true Web 2.0 fashion, Second Life is virtually unregulated and unsupervised, it has become a channel for all kinds of social and ethical vices. Though there are (largely unenforced) rules against inappropriate behavior in public (virtual) spaces, users can act out all of their most base or prurient instincts in virtual private. For 220 Linden dollars, one can even act out virtual rape fantasies; options include "rape victim," "get raped," or "hold victim."[12]

"But it's just a game," some users protest. Sure. A game so all-consuming that many of its users spend up to twelve hours a day online running their virtual businesses, spending time with their virtual families, and tending to their virtual homes, ceasing to be functioning, productive members of society.

"The Internet problem is still in its infancy," Dr. Elias Aboujaoude, the principal author of the October 2006 Stanford study on online addiction, admitted.

So what will the world look like in 2020 if nothing is done to rein in addictions of an online culture?

Baroness Susan Greenfield, a member of the British House of Lords and a professor of Neuroscience at Oxford University, argues that the consequences for the future generation are grave. Her research indicates that the ubiquity of digital technology is altering the shape and chemistry of our brains, and that violent video games and intense online interactivity can generate mental disorders such as autism, attention deficit disorder, and hyperactivity. Thus children of the Web 2.0 generation, she suggests, will be more prone to real-world violence, less able to compromise or negotiate, apt to be poor learners, and lacking in empathy.

A scary vision of the future, indeed.

From hypersexed teenagers, to identity thieves, to compulsive gamblers and addicts of all stripes, the moral fabric of our society is being unraveled by Web 2.0. It seduces us into acting on our most deviant instincts and allows us to succumb to our most destructive vices. And it is corroding and corrupting the values we share as a nation.

7

1984
(version 2.0)

Everybody Knows

t began as a moral dilemma. *Should you plan sex before meeting a cyber lover?* she asked the search engine on April 17, 2006.

The problem was that she was *married but in love with another man,* as she confessed to the search engine on April 20.

A week later, she had made up her mind to meet her Internet lover. *What do men think is sexy?* she inquired ten days later as she finalized her plans—the plane tickets, the hotel and restaurant reservations—to fly from her home in Houston to meet him in San Antonio.

She spent the night of May 4 with him in San Antonio's Omni Hotel. It was a disaster. *i met my cyber lover and the sex was not good,* she confessed on May 8. *Online friend is horrible in person.*

Does God punish adultery? she asked on May 13.

How do I know all these intimate details about a stranger?

I know it because I've read her entries on her AOL search engine. I've scanned every entry she made between March 1, 2006, and May 31, 2006.

She had opened her heart to this technology, transforming her search-engine queries into a window to her soul. She's as real as lonelygirl15, the fictionalized actress on YouTube, is fake. The thoughts and feelings that she poured into AOL's search engine reveal a woman struggling to maintain her sanity in the face of despair.

From March through the end of May, she fed 2,393 questions into the search engine—questions that she would have been too shy to ask even her closest friends; questions about her body, male sexuality, Internet addiction, and God's justice. She was a digital *Madame Bovary,* with just one caveat—her entries in the AOL search engine weren't intended to be published. There was no Flaubert behind her confessions. They weren't supposed to be read by anyone. She trusted her search engine absolutely. Amid her snoring spouse, her invisible children, her heartbreaking adultery, her struggle to make sense of God's word, it was her sole confidante, the one certainty that could never let her down.

How wrong she was. Her utter frankness with the

search engine represented her most serious misjudgment, one even more misguided than her decision to spend the night with her Internet lover. For soon the Internet turned her into a global media celebrity. Her search engine entries between March and May—all 2,393 of them—would be released on the Internet for public consumption. Her confessions would be read and "interpreted" by thousands of voyeuristic bloggers. Little did AOL user #711391 know that she would become one of the first casualties of a digital surveillance culture in which our deepest fears and most intimate emotions can be broadcast, *without our knowledge or permission,* to the world.

Everybody knows her now, including, no doubt, some Houston neighbors who could tell us her name, her address, and the ages of her kids. We now know this Texan woman as intimately as we know our own spouse—her bedroom attire (*purple lingerie*), her body flaws (*can spider veins swell up and turn red?*), the color of her pubic hair (*blond*), and her post-adultery wisdom (*don't ever have sex with your best friend*).

The online magazine *Slate* described the release of her entries as a flagrant invasion of fundamental individual rights. It was, the magazine claimed, "Orwellian."

As so it is. Welcome to 1984, version 2.0.

Our new Orwellian age got its public screening on the evening of Sunday, August 6, 2006, when AOL leaked the search data of 658,000 people (including AOL user #711391). Critics immediately dubbed this information leak "Data Valdez," after the 1989 *Exxon Valdez* oil tanker spill. Twenty-three million of the AOL users' most private thoughts—on everything from abortions and killing one's spouse to bestiality and pedophilia—were spilled on the Internet to the world without their knowledge or permission.

All this data became the intellectual plaything of AOL researchers—not surprising in an industry where search companies like Google and Yahoo treat the billions of queries in their search engines as their own property, to store, analyze, and profit from.

But the legal ownership of search-engine queries remains murky. Marc Rotenberg, the executive director of the Electronic Privacy Information Center, described it as a "ticking privacy time bomb." That bomb exploded on August 6, when AOL researchers accidentally posted the database of queries online. Hackers promptly downloaded this data and "democratically" distributed it across the Web. Now anyone—workmates, friends, and family, of course, as well as blackmailers and other cybercriminals—could pore through this enormous database of private intentions.

It was the equivalent of the Catholic Church mailing out 658,000 confessions to its worldwide parishioners. Or the KGB, the Soviet secret police, throwing open their surveillance files and broadcasting them on national television.

The information in these AOL files is a twenty-first-century version of *Notes from Underground*—replete with information that reveals us at our most vulnerable, our most private, our most shameful, our most human. They include every imaginable query, from *"how to kill your wife"* and *"I want revenge for my wife"* to *"losing your virginity," "can you still be pregnant even though your period came?"* and *"can you not get pregnant by having sex without a condom?"*

"My goodness, it's my whole personal life," a sixty-two-year-old widow from Georgia told the *New York Times*, horrified, when she learned that her personal life had been splayed across the Internet. "I had no idea somebody was looking over my shoulder."

Of course, this was far from being the only major privacy debacle of the digital age. In February 2005, scam artists broke into the databases at ChoicePoint, an Atlanta-based data broker, which, MSNBC reports, maintains background information on almost every U.S. citizen. This breach, in which identity thieves obtained data through the fake accounts they had set up by posing as legitimate clients, exposed over 163,000 financial records and resulted in close to 800 cases of identity theft. "We believe that several individuals, posing as legitimate business customers, recently committed fraud by claiming to have a lawful purpose for accessing information about individuals," ChoicePoint told its shocked victims. "You should continue to check your credit reports frequently for the next year."

In May 2006, a couple of teenagers stole a laptop from the Department of Veterans Affairs, leaking the financial histories of 25 million veterans. And then there were the hackers who, in September 2006, broke into the Second Life database and stole the real-life records—including names, addresses, contact information, and financial information—of its 600,000 virtual inhabitants.

Worse still, the data from 40 million MasterCard and Visa accounts was stolen in July 2005. Just think about that the next time you enter your credit card number on an online shopping site.

And with doctors and hospitals increasingly storing their records online (on sites like WebMD.com), medical records, too—which can include anything from prescription-drug information, to surgical histories, to treatments for sexually transmitted disease—can easily fall into the wrong hands. In one recent case, records of 260,000 patients in Indiana were compromised when an outside contractor downloaded the records onto CDs and placed them in a computer bag, which he later returned to the store with the CDs still inside.[1] In cases like these, consequences go beyond mere embarrassment or invasion of privacy. According to the *San Diego Business Journal*, there are over 200,000 medical identity-theft cases each year, and that number is on the rise.[2] With just a fraudulent Social Security number or a stolen insurance card (easily obtained by even an amateur hacker), thieves can amass thousands of dollars in medical bills, create legal liabilities by submitting fraudulent insurance claims, or tamper with existing records in such a way that jeopardizes future insurance coverage.

The consequences of a stolen identity on the Web can perhaps best be seen in the following story of a man who had his life turned upside down for two years.

There are two kinds of guys in the world: those who own their own tuxedo and those who rent.

Paul Fairchild falls firmly into the latter category. A thirty-four-year-old Web developer from the bedroom community of Edmond, Oklahoma, with a wife and two small kids, Fairchild is the quintessential renter. He rents his small ranch-style home in the little suburb of Oklahoma City. And he also rents his tuxedos when he needs to, which, given his modest lifestyle, is rarely.

In the summer of 2003, Paul Fairchild had good reason to rent a tux. His sister was getting married in Portland, Oregon. Having cobbled together the money to fly his family out to the wedding, Fairchild went to a local tuxedo rental store to outfit himself for the ceremony.

Do you take American Express?

Sure.

The assistant took Fairchild's credit card to process the rental, but reappeared a few minutes later, looking slightly flustered.

Excuse me, sir, but your card has been declined.

Paul Fairchild didn't understand it. He rarely used his American Express card. Money was tight in the Fairchild household—so tight, indeed, that his family could barely afford the $12 shoes from Payless that he and his wife bought for their son to wear at the wedding.

He called customer service. Your account is delinquent, a woman told him.

That's impossible, he said.

Are you the sole proprietor?

Huh?

The sole proprietor, she repeated. Of the Ebony Passion Escort Service in Brooklyn, New York. That's you, right?

I'm afraid there must be some mistake.

There had been a mistake. A huge one.

Paul Fairchild's identity, including a false ID displaying his genuine photograph, had, so to speak, been digitally rented. It had been borrowed without his permission or knowledge by the proprietor of the Ebony Passion Escort Service, a prostitution service that operated out of Brooklyn, New York.

There was another Paul Fairchild. A fake East Coast version, the kind of guy who buys rather than rents tuxedos using other people's credit cards. He was an identity thief, a flesh-shop operator who had run up over $500,000 in debts on credit cards, cell-phone and car-rental bills, as well as a store account with a New York jewelry wholesaler. On this Fairchild credit card, instead of a $12 charge for shoes from Payless, there was a $750 charge for Manolo Blahnik footwear, as well as charges for furs and diamonds, and a $500 charge for high-end tobacco. Most egregiously, this Paul Fairchild had committed to a mortgage of $315,000 for an apartment building in downtown Brooklyn—an operational center, no doubt, for his escort service.

For the real Fairchild, the consequences of the theft were, to quote the *New York Times,* "two years of hell." He spent forty hours a week for the first four months after the revelation of the identity theft just dealing with police reports and filing notarized affidavits to each defrauded company. Extracting himself from the mortgage proved particularly time-consuming and expensive. Wells Fargo Bank, one of the owners of the debt, ended up suing Fairchild, who was forced to hire a lawyer to defend himself. Even two years after the identity theft was exposed, he was still getting billed by telephone companies for charges racked up by the fraudster.[5]

Meanwhile, the fake Fairchild, the owner of Ebony Passion Escort Service, remains on the loose. And there's little chance of catching him. Of the estimated ten million identity thefts each year, it is estimated that only one in 700 are ever apprehended.

The only good news is that Paul Fairchild is now the one and only Paul Fairchild. And he's still that modest guy from Oklahoma who rents, rather than owns, a tuxedo. Even more so now. You see, since the identity theft, his credit rating has been hit hard and his credit limits have been severely cut. So it might be a stretch to afford the rental on a tux next time somebody in his family gets married.

What is in many ways more shocking than the amount of stolen information on the Web is the amount of private information traded *legally* on the Internet each day.

In July 2006, Google performed 2.7 billion and Yahoo performed 1.8 billion unique searches. In the Web 2.0 world, where each and every one of these searches is readily available to corporations or government agencies, the right to privacy is becoming an antiquated notion. In the physical world, we can tear up bank statements and phone bills, discard private notes or letters, shred embarrassing photos, or keep our medical records under lock and key. But once immortalized by AOL or Google, our online records are here to stay.

Google, Yahoo, and AOL, who have no legal responsibility to purge old data, keep records of what subjects we search, what products we buy, what sites we surf. These search engines want to know us intimately, they want to be our closest confidante. You see, the more information they possess about us—our hobbies, our tastes, and our desires—the more information they can sell advertisers and marketers, allowing them to better personalize their products, pitches, and approaches. But our information is not distributed to advertisers alone. Everyone from hackers to cyberthieves to state and federal officials can potentially find out anything from the last movie ticket we bought, to the prescription medications we're taking, to the balance of our savings account.

So how do Google and AOL acquire such detailed information? Through the innocently named "cookies"—tiny parcels of data embedded in our Internet browser that establish a unique ID number on our hard disk and enable Web sites to collect precise records of

1984 (version 2.0)

everything we do online. These data parcels represent a Faustian pact made with the Internet devil. Each time we land on a Web page, a cookie is activated, telling that site who is visiting it. Cookies transform our habits into data. They are gold mines for marketers and advertisers. They record our site preferences, they remember our credit card information, they store what we put into our electronic shopping carts, and they note which banner advertisements we click on.

And they are everywhere.

How long do these cookies last? The life span of each company's cookie differs. Google's cookie, for example, doesn't expire until 2036. (In March 2007, they changed that policy for new searches.) It is possible to disable the use of cookies on your computer; but as the so-called "Yahoo Privacy Center" warns all users:

> If you reject all cookies, you will not be able to use
> Yahoo! Products or services that require you to "sign
> in" and you may not be able to take full advantage
> of all offerings.

No cookies, no Yahoo! Mail, no personalized My Yahoo! Homepage, none of the digital goodies that our friends at Yahoo give us for free. From my own My Yahoo! page, the company knows that I live in Berkeley, go to the movies a lot, read the *New York Times,* and follow an English soccer club called Tottenham Hotspur. Meanwhile, my g-mail account, which is scanning all my e-mails for key words that it uses to generate customized advertisements, knows that I'm planning a trip to New York City on JetBlue, pre-ordered a copy of *The Long Tail* on Amazon, and subscribe to BMG's classical music club. Everything I do and everywhere I go on the Internet is recorded by somebody for some commercial end.

This compilation of personal information is not just limited to the Internet search engines. On August 10, 2006, four days after AOL's release of its search queries, the Internet retail giant Amazon.com lodged a request with the United States Patent and Trademark Office to patent "a system to gather and keep massive amounts of intimate information about its millions of shoppers." This "system" is designed to compile the most intimate economic, ethnic, sexual, and religious information about Amazon shoppers. Amazon not only wants to own our online shopping experience, they want to own the online shopper—turning each of us into another data point within an infinite database of e-commerce intentions.

Sir Francis Bacon, the Elizabethan father of inductive science, wrote optimistically that "knowledge is power." But in our contemporary digital age, it is information, rather than knowledge, that lends power. And the more personal the information, the more power it promises to those who hold it.

The age of surveillance is not just being imposed from above by the aggregators of data. It's also being driven from below by our own self-broadcasting obsession. The

Web 2.0's infatuation with user-generated content is a data miner's dream. The more we reveal about ourselves on our MySpace page, in our YouTube videos, on our blog, or on the blogs of others, the more vulnerable we become to snoops, blackmailers, voyeurs, and gossips. The confessional nature of user-generated culture is resulting in a cultural explosion of personal, sexual, and political self-revelation.

Privacy is no longer cool. Just look at the high traffic on sites such as DailyConfession.com, NotProud.com, and PostSecret.com, which are made up of anonymous confessions of everything from greed to slothfulness to insatiable lust. It is a haven for voyeurs—a place where people can go to poke their noses into other people's business. And while ostensibly anonymous, these sites, of course, all use cookies to identify both readers and writers. How long will it be before somebody hacks into one of these sites and leaks the names and addresses of all the confessors?

Not surprisingly, the Central Intelligence Agency— that government-funded organization of official nose-pokers—is now investing in Web 2.0 technology. The CIA has embraced something it calls "spy-blogging," which involves the spooks sharing one another's research, aerial photographs, and secret videos.

To justify spy-blogging, one defense expert at the Naval Postgraduate School, parodying Orwellian doublespeak, told the *New York Times*, "To fight a network like al Qaeda, you have to behave like a network."[4] Next thing, they'll be telling us that to beat the terrorists, they have to fly planes into tall buildings.

According to the *New York Times*, the wisdom-of-the-crowd premise of the CIA's spy-blogging initiative is that "a million connected amateurs will always be smarter than a few experts collected in an elite star chamber."

That's a very large crowd of democratically organized secret policemen. I just hope that they aren't sharing information about my private life with a million of their closest colleagues.

This democratized, user-generated media, where everyone gets to spy on everyone else, represents the collective implosion of our privacy rights. In this digital panopticon, teachers watch the kids, college administrators watch the students, and peers watch peers. Orwell's *Nineteen Eighty-Four* painted a picture of a top-down surveillance society where Big Brother sees everything, knows all, watches our movements, listens to our conversations, and reads our minds. Well, the Web 2.0 is the democratization of that Orwellian nightmare; instead of a single all-seeing, all-knowing Orwellian leader, now anyone can be Big Brother. All you need is an Internet connection.

And maybe a digital camera. At HollaBackNYC.com, for example, users are invited to "holla back at street harassers" by taking their photo and then posting them online. HollabackNYC now has popular sister sites in many American cities, as well as in Canada and Europe, where users post photos of people supposedly ogling them in the street. So the next time you flash someone on the street a friendly smile, be prepared for them to snap your photo and make you an involuntary member of the HollaBack community. It's an ideal way to publicly humiliate innocent people trying to mind their own business and live their lives.

It's not just sites like HollaBack that are transforming citizens into snoops. In December 2006, Reuters and Yahoo introduced an online initiative to feature amateur videos and photographs on both their Web sites. Reuters also plans on distributing these images to the many thousands of broadcast, online, and print media subscribers to their news service.

"What if everybody in the world were my stringers?" the president of Reuters media group told the *New York Times* in December 2006 without, it seems, any hint of irony.

What if, indeed. This Reuters and Yahoo partnership encourages anyone to take photographs of anybody else in the vague guise of news.

"There is an ongoing demand for interesting and iconic images," the Reuters president explained, justifying this initiative of transforming anyone with a camera into paparazzi.

But who gives who permission to take *interesting* and *iconic* photos? When does this sort of citizen journalism become intrusive? And who is to distinguish between a tasteless prying into other people's lives and the genuine pursuit of news?

From our entries on search engines, to the content of our e-mails, to our blog postings, to the insalubrious details we post about ourselves on social-networking sites, the Web 2.0 revolution is blurring the lines between public and private.

What happens when all our queries and postings and casual comments become open to public consumption, and the Web becomes a permanent repository of the details of our lives? Our rights to free expression are jeopardized.

Do you think for a moment that what is posted by or about you doesn't matter? Think again. Reed College denied admission to a student in 2006 because he had posted rude comments about the college on his LiveJournal blog. Twenty students at a middle school in Costa Mesa, California, were suspended for making anti-Semitic remarks in a MySpace group. Athletes at Louisiana Sate and the University of Colorado were suspended for rude remarks on Facebook about their coach. And a graduating senior at Vermont Technical College had a job offer rescinded after the employer saw references to partying and alcohol on the student's Facebook page.

In the fall of 2006, Aleksey Vayner, a senior at Yale, applied for a job at the Swiss investment bank UBS; he also submitted a detailed résumé, an eleven-page cover letter, and a self-made video entitled "Impossible is nothing," which showed off his bench-pressing and tennis-playing prowess. Somebody at UBS put Vayner's application materials online and his video on YouTube;

within days, he was getting hundreds of derisive and even threatening e-mails. The digital lynch mob ended Vayner's career in banking before he'd set foot in Zurich. Now the Yale senior is considering a job in real estate.

The public humiliation of Aleksey Vayner or the AOL users can't, however, compare to the experience of thirty-seven-year-old Chinese dissident journalist Shi Tao. In April 2005, Tao, who reported for *Contemporary Business News* in Hunan Province, was sentenced to ten years in prison by a Chinese court for "illegally providing state secrets to foreign entities." His crime? He'd e-mailed some Western correspondents information about the Chinese government's media coverage of the fifteenth anniversary of the Tiananmen Square massacre. Shi Tao was caught when Yahoo provided the Chinese government with information that traced the dissident through his e-mail account and personal computer.

The Ultimate Search Engine

Big Brother is very much alive and well in the Silicon Valley town of Mountain View, California. It is here that Google, the world's most powerful Web 2.0 company, has its global HQ. And it is out of their offices that the dawn of digital surveillance is being built, algorithm by algorithm, by an army of the world's leading engineers, mathematicians, and software architects.

According to Nigel Gilbert, a professor at Surrey University and head of a 2006 Royal Academy study into surveillance, Google is within five years of having sufficient information to be able to track the exact movements and intentions of every individual, via Google Earth (which can already be used by foreign governments to pinpoint exact locations of secret U.S. army bases), Google Calendar, or the new Web site currently under development, Google Health.[5]

Gilbert's concerns are shared by the UK's Information Commissioner, Richard Thomas, who wrote, "I fear that we are waking up to a surveillance society that is already all around us." It is an apprehension that has also been echoed by a number of leading American critics, including Adam Greenfield, the author of *Everyware: The Dawning Age of Ubiquitous Computing.*

In the short-term future, Greenfield predicts, small computers will become embedded in everything from clothes to beer mats. The consequence of his "Everyware" scenario will be a world in which we, as citizens, will be interfacing with computers in everything we do, from meeting chip-wearing strangers on the street to drinking an intelligent pint of beer. Each of our daily interfaces with smart buildings, smart furniture, smart clothing, or even smart bathtubs will produce data, and all this information will end up in a Google-like database—the database to end all databases.

Everyware represents the real dawn of the age of surveillance. Once computers exist in clothing, on walls and streets, in living rooms and bathrooms, then absolutely everything is knowable. All this information can be collected, networked, and distributed. As Professor Gilbert says, we will be able to type into Google, "What was a particular individual doing at 2:30 yesterday? and would get an answer."

It is a world without privacy, a world in which individuals are turned inside out.

According to the *New York Times*, the next Web boom (3.0, if you will) is likely to be driven by "intelligent" software that can use information from the Web to intuit our future decisions and intentions. A University of Washington project called KnowItAll, for example (funded by none other than Google), has rolled out a test software that can mine databases of online hotel reviews and link them to past customer preferences, then use cognitive deduction to find the best hotel for each individual user. This may seem unthreatening at first glance. After all, who wouldn't want a computer to pick out the hotel with the most convenient location, the best swimming pool, and a room-service menu serving our favorite dish? But do we really want to open the door to technology that takes the place of human reasoning and individual decision-making? Do we really want Google to know enough about us that they can anticipate our actions and predict our ways of thinking?

Google, with its Ministry of Truth credo of *Do No Evil*, is leading the charge into this brave new world of ubiquitous information. Speaking at the appropriately named "Zeitgeist '06" conference for Google's European partners, Google cofounder Larry Page imagined the "ultimate" search engine.[6]

"The ultimate search engine would understand everything in the world. It would understand everything that you asked it and give you back the exact right thing instantly."

Page's "ultimate search engine" is Google's holy grail. It's the modern-day version of the ancient Greek oracle. It's the Judeo-Christian idea of an omnipotent, omnipresent God.

So what happens to the human beings of the future who must coexist with Google's ultimate database? What becomes of us in an age of total digital surveillance?

Everybody knows.

8

solutions

So what is to be done?

How can we channel the Web 2.0 revolution constructively, so that it enriches rather than undermines our economy, culture, and values? What can we do to ensure that our most valuable traditions—celebrating knowledge and expertise, fostering creative achievement, sustaining and supporting a reliable and prosperous information economy—aren't swept away by the tsunami of the cult of the amateur?

I'm neither antitechnology nor antiprogress. Digital technology is a miraculous thing, giving us the means to globally connect and share knowledge in unprecedented ways. This book certainly couldn't have been completed without e-mail or the Internet, and I'm the last person to romanticize a past in which we wrote letters by candlelight and had them delivered by Pony Express.

Digital technology has become an inescapable part of twenty-first-century life. Kevin Kelly told Silicon Valley's TED Conference in February 2005, "You can delay technology, but you can't stop it." And that is true. For better or for worse, Web 2.0 participatory media is reshaping our intellectual, political, and commercial landscape. We can't outlaw Wikipedia, or resurrect Tower Records, or change the realities that have made sites like MySpace and YouTube enormously popular and increasingly profitable. Our challenge, instead, is to protect the legacy of our mainstream media and two hundred years of copyright protections within the context of twenty-first-century digital technology. Our goal should be to preserve our culture and our values, while enjoying the benefits of today's Internet capabilities. We need to find a way to balance the best of the digital future without destroying the institutions of the past.

Citizendium

In January 2000, thirty-year-old doctoral student Larry Sanger came to Internet entrepreneur Jimmy Wales with the idea of building a cultural blog. As I've described in Chapter 2, Wales hired Sanger, and the two men first created a peer-reviewed encyclopedia called Nupedia, then, in January 2001, founded Wikipedia.

But unlike Sergei Brin and Larry Page at Google, or Steve Chen and Chad Hurley at YouTube, the Wales-Sanger partnership didn't have a happy ending.

Why? Because Larry Sanger came to his senses about Wikipedia. He recognized the appallingly destructive consequences of the Wikipedia experiment. Sanger ran Wikipedia's day-to-day operations. He was responsible for policing the lunatic-fringe amateurs who posted and reposted thousands of entries a day. After two years, he had had enough of anonymous anarchists like "the Cunctator" and their ceaseless debates and bickering over Wikipedia controls and quality.

The lesson Sanger drew from his experience at Wikipedia is that the democratization of information can quickly degenerate into an intellectually corrosive radical egalitarianism. The knowledge of the expert, in fact, *does* trump the collective "wisdom" of amateurs. He learned that an open-source encyclopedia like Wikipedia could only function effectively if it reserved some authority to screen and edit its anonymous contributions. He learned that fully democratic open-source networks inevitably get corrupted by loonies.

Wikipedia's problem, Sanger realized, was with its implementation, not its technology. So he went away and rethought how to incorporate the voice and authority of experts with the user-generated content. And he returned with a solution that incorporates the best of old and new media.

He called it Citizendium. Launched in September

2006, Sanger describes it as "an experimental new wiki project that combines public participation with gentle expert guidance." In other words, it is an attempt to fuse the strengths of a trusted resource like the *Encyclopaedia Britannica* with the participatory energy of Wikipedia. On Citizendium, experts in specific subjects have the power to review, approve, and settle disputes about articles within their intellectual specialty. A select group of "constables" maintain order on the site by censoring rule-breakers and troublemakers.

What is so refreshing about Citizendium is that it acknowledges the fact that some people know more about certain things than others—that the Harvard English professor does, in fact, know more about literature and its evolution than a high school kid. If even a Web 2.0 pioneer like Larry Sanger can come to recognize this, maybe there is hope after all for the user-generated Web 2.0.

Larry Sanger is not the only Web 2.0 pioneer who has come to his senses about the inferiority of amateur content. Niklas Zennstrom and Janus Friis, the founders of the original file-sharing service Kazaa as well as the online telephony company Skype (which they sold to eBay for $2.5 billion in September 2005), have launched Joost, a new digital media initiative for a world in which the Internet and television are rapidly converging. Joost is a service that promises to provide professional creators of video with a peer-to-peer platform for distributing and selling their content over the Internet. The platform will enable professional content producers to combine the traditional one-to-many broadcasting functionality of network television with the many-to-many interactivity of online content. A second television platform that offers the similar promise is Brightcove, a Boston-based start-up founded by former Macromedia chief technology officer Jeremy Allaire, which, by January 2007, had raised $60 million in venture capital.

"TV is 507 channels and nothing on and we want to change that!" Friis—borrowing a Springsteen verse—wrote.

But the alternative to 507 channels doesn't have to be 507 million channels. Unlike user-generated content services such as YouTube, platforms like Joost and Brightcove maintain the all-important division between content creators and content consumers. They are designed to enable professional creators of video content to deliver high-quality, interactive content to both the personal computer and the television (thus Viacom's decision, in February 2007, to license some of its MTV, Comedy Central, and BET programming to Joost). These next-generation platforms will offer the best of both the old and new media worlds—enabling us to simultaneously video chat and instant message with one another while watching our favorite shows. In 1990, technology visionary George Gilder published *Life After Television*. With exciting new technology companies like Joost and Brightcove, the world after TV can really begin to take shape.

This gives me hope that the Web 2.0 technology can be used to empower, rather than overshadow, the authority of the expert, that the digital revolution might usher in an age in which the authority of the expert is strengthened. Take, for example, a site called iAmplify—a publishing platform that allows professionals to sell audio or video downloads that offer instruction and expertise (in everything from weight-loss to finance to parenting) directly to the site's subscribers. iAmplify shows how Web 2.0 technology can provide professionals with more direct channels to reach their market.

So is the future iAmplify or MySpace? Is it YouTube or Joost? Wikipedia or Citizendium? The question is ideological rather than technological—and the answer is largely up to us. We can—and must—resist the siren song of the noble amateur and use Web 2.0 to put trust in our experts again.

Many traditional newspapers and magazines, too, are responding to the challenges they face by marrying new media and traditional content without compromising editorial standards or quality.

One such institution is the left-of-center British newspaper the *Guardian*, which has managed to shift a portion of its business online while still maintaining its high-quality news gathering and reporting. Its online version, *Guardian Unlimited*, has done such a brilliant job of integrating the authoritative traditions of the newspaper with the interactive democracy of the Web 2.0 world that it now boasts more online readers in the United States than such top domestic newspapers as the *Los Angeles Times*. Sure, the *Guardian Unlimited* has anonymous message boards littered with uninformed, unregulated, reader-generated opinions. But unlike many online editions, where readers' blogs and paid advertisements are indistinguishable from actual articles, on the *Guardian Unlimited*, the division between professional reportage and amateur opinion is clearly delineated.

And though the *Guardian Unlimited* is free, it has managed to achieve some measure of economic success by effectively balancing its costs with its online advertising sales. The good news is that other print newspapers are now following the *Guardian*'s embrace of the online medium. In January 2007, for example, the new editor of the *Los Angeles Times*, James E. O'Shea, launched a high-profile initiative to invest significantly more resources in digital technology and online reporting, particularly in the coverage of "hyper local" news. O'Shea's goal was to more cost-effectively deliver the news to his readers—what he described as the "daily bread of democracy."[1]

Recently, the *Wall Street Journal* decided to move some of its analysis and opinion online as well, reducing the size and cost of the paper edition but without compromising its news-gathering ability or journalistic integrity. Such success gives one hope that newspapers can simultaneously embrace the online medium, maintain their professional standards, enlarge readership, and increase revenues.

The Internet is also maturing as a medium for professionally produced news sites. The January 2007 launch of *Politico*, a Washington, D.C., based online news publication, proves that professional journalism is suited to the more flexible and informal medium of the Internet. Founded by John Harris, former political editor of the *Washington Post*, *Politico* is staffed by well-trained journalists from publications such as the *Washington Post*, *Time* magazine, National Public Radio, and *Bloomberg News*. These A-list journalists will bring to the Web start-up not only credibility and name recognition, but also the ethical standards, inside-the-Beltway network, and institutional knowledge lent by their successful careers in traditional media.

And in November 2006, Arianna Huffington, the charismatic Southern Californian impresario behind the eponymous HuffingtonPost.com, announced that she would be hiring professional journalists from publications like the *New York Times* and *Newsweek* to report on Congress and the 2008 presidential elections for her blog, adding news-reporting capability to the mix of opinion and commentary. As a result, the Huffington Post will enjoy the best of both worlds—the immediacy and energy of a blog site with original, quality reportage. Still, a handful of reporters covering politics and the elections hardly replaces a full-scale newspaper in the breadth and scope of its reporting. At the end of the day, perhaps the long-term viability of our media depends upon the actions and behaviors of each of us. If we agree with the notion of a free press and strong news-gathering media, we need to support it by continuing to subscribe to and read the papers. Nothing is more important in a democracy such as ours than an informed citizenship. In the meantime, the news organizations, too, are trying to adapt and change.

As advertising dollars migrate to the Web, more newspapers are attempting to boost ad revenue through strategic partnerships with online businesses. In November 2006, Yahoo formed a partnership with 176 daily newspapers by which the papers' classified ads could be accessed through the Yahoo site. That month, Google announced a similar deal, agreeing to share content, advertising, and technology with a group of fifty major newspapers, including the *Washington Post*, the *Chicago Tribune*, and the *New York Times*. Monster.com, the online career site, has agreed to post job listings from forty national newspapers, including the *Philadelphia Enquirer* and the *Philadelphia Daily News*. The question is whether such partnerships help newspapers generate enough ad dollars to make up for plunging circulations.

And what of the music industry? Can music companies rethink their business models to stay competitive despite the surge in digital downloading and piracy? According to the *New York Times*, cost-analysis data on a successful hip-hop record recently released by Warner Records revealed that only 74 percent of the total revenue from the release came from actual CD sales—the rest was from the sale of ring tones, related cell-phone games, and cell-phone wallpaper and screen backgrounds. Clearly, there is money to be made in digital products tied to album releases. In other parts of the world, the sale of digital add-ons is even more profitable. Can the music industry find ways to make enough money off such products to make up for the lost revenue from piracy?

It continues to astound me each time I walk into Amoeba, one of the few local record stores left in Berkeley, that a newly released CD, on average, still costs $16. When consumers can get an album on iTunes for $10, or cherry-pick individual songs for a dollar, why does the music industry cling to its archaic pricing structure? The industry should find ways of streamlining the costs of packaging, storing, and distributing physical albums so that CD prices can become more competitive with digital albums. Sure, that is not the end-all and be-all with regard to piracy, but such a gesture could be a first step in the fight to win back its customers.

It is also astounding that the big labels cling to their faith in the power of digital rights management software (DRM) to somehow magically stem the tide of digital piracy. DRM is the copy-protection software that comes with the downloaded music sold by the big labels, blocking us from easily transferring our legally pur chased digital music from our Apple iPod player to other players, and from our iTunes jukebox to our Napster or Real Networks libraries. But what the recent history of the music business clearly demonstrates is that thieves steal music online no matter what intricate digital electronic lock is supposed to be protecting it. This may be why even Apple CEO Steve Jobs—whose brilliantly designed iPod player and iTunes store have pioneered the growth of digital music into a $2 billion global market in 2006[2]—has come out against DRM. Given that the Apple iTunes store sold around 85 percent of the legal 525 million digital music downloads bought in the United States in 2006,[3] Jobs' controversial position is certainly something that the record industry should contemplate carefully. In a February 2007 essay, the Apple CEO wrote that the vast majority of today's digital piracy stems from illegally traded music copied from compact discs (which are DRM-free) rather than from digital downloads. What does Jobs conclude are the benefits of DRM? "There appear to be none," he says.[4]

Once again, it is we, the consumers of music, who play a role in this ongoing saga. We have to understand that the illegal downloading and sharing of music is killing off an industry that has treated us to recordings by everyone from Paul Simon and the Beatles to Beyoncé and Carrie Underwood. A viable future of the music business lies somewhere between that $16 compact disc and the free, stolen digital file. One potential version of this future lies with eMusic, the new big player in the digital music business (second only to Apple). eMusic sells DRM-free music files in the MP3 format, which means its subscribers can download songs into any digital player or jukebox. Although the four big labels have so far resisted including their catalogs on the eMusic service, the site nonetheless boasts 250,000 subscribers who pay $9.99 per month to download thirty songs selected from the 11,000 independent labels who sell their catalogs on the site.[5] And in the third quarter of 2006, it recorded a 10 percent share of the entire digital music market—the same as the total share of Napster, MSN Music and Yahoo Music combined. The success of eMusic's business model shows that consumers are willing to pay for music when it is competitively priced and easy to buy. And eMusic's successful aggregation of catalogs from 11,000 independent labels suggests that the labels and artists *can* still make money by selling their music at significantly less than 99 cents a track. eMusic paints a hopeful picture that a vibrant recorded music industry and satisfied music consumers *can* coexist in the digital future. In February 2007, one of the big four labels—EMI—was rumored to be wrestling with the idea of releasing their catalog in the MP3 format.[6] So perhaps by the time you read this, one or more of the big labels will have taken that all-important first plunge into a DRM-free digital world.

The way to keep the recorded-music industry vibrant is to be willing to support new bands and music, and new services like eMusic, with our dollars—to stop stealing the sweat of other people's creative labor.

Crime and Punishment

In March 2006, I became embroiled in an online debate with Instapundit blogger Glenn Reynolds about morality. In reviewing his book, *Army of Davids* for the *Weekly Standard,* I argued that Reynolds, in the romantic tradition of Marx, had invested an unreasonable level of trust in mankind's ability to use technology responsibly.

But this is the key question in the debate between pragmatists like myself (or so I like to think) and digital utopians like Reynolds. Can we really trust society to behave properly in the Wild West culture of the Web 2.0 revolution?

I would argue that we are easily seduced, corrupted, and led astray. In other words, we need rules and regulations to help control our behavior online, just as we need traffic laws to regulate how we drive in order to protect everyone from accidents. Sometimes it takes government regulation to protect us from our worst instincts and most self-destructive behavior. The fact is, modest regulation of the Internet works. Let me give you an example.

On Sunday, July 15, 2006, David Carruthers, a smartly attired British executive in his late forties with wire-rimmed glasses and a balding pate, and his wife, Carol, were changing planes at the Dallas–Fort Worth International Airport on their way from London to San José, Costa Rica. But as it happened, he never made it to Costa Rica. Before he could board American Airlines flight 2167, he was arrested and detained by federal authorities under charges of racketeering, conspiracy, and fraud.

Carruthers was the CEO of BetonSports, an online gambling company publicly traded on the London Stock Exchange, which, in 2005, earned $20.1 million in profits on $1.77 billion revenue. Although online gambling is prohibited in the United States under the 1961 Federal Wire Act, which forbids the use of wire communication (including the Internet) for the transmission of bets or

the cult of the amateur

196

wagers, casino businesses like BetonSports, 888.com, SportingBet, and PartyGaming have nevertheless sprung up, generating about $6 billion in revenue from Americans betting on everything from football to poker to roulette. Until now, these companies got around the American justice system by locating their computer servers offshore in tax-free Costa Rica, Gibraltar, Antigua, or the Channel Islands, where they managed to operate largely off the radar of the American authorities.

The arrest of David Carruthers at DFW Airport, and the subsequent arrest of another online gambling kingpin, Peter Dicks, the chairman of SportingBet, a few months later, dealt a swift blow to the illegal online betting business. With its CEO sitting in a Dallas courtroom in his prison-issued orange jumpsuit and facing a twenty-two-count criminal indictment, BetonSports stopped accepting bets from users with American IP addresses, and SportingBet has sold off its entire U.S. operation.

More recent congressional legislation has helped curb illegal gambling operations further. On September 30, 2006, Congress passed the Unlawful Internet Gambling Enforcement Act, which created new criminal penalties for banks and credit card companies that process payments to online gambling companies. And in January 2007, indictments were handed down to four major investment firms for underwriting the initial public offerings of online gambling operations.

Strong legislation and effective law enforcement *can* be

solutions

effective. The number of online casinos has been reduced. And according to *The Economist* magazine, the 2006 legislation "proved enough to cripple an industry already reeling from the earlier arrests," prompting PartyGaming to immediately halt its U.S. business. But the government still needs to continue to legislate against online gambling and go after and shut down offshore gambling businesses.

Gambling is not the only Internet activity that would benefit from more regulation. I feel we need the same uncompromising crackdown on online fraud, identity theft, and the unbridled stealing of intellectual property.

In February 2006, Massachusetts congressman Ed Markey introduced a bill requiring search-engine companies to delete any information about visitors that is not required for legitimate business purposes. It is a step in the right direction. Only by putting legal limitations on the type of data that can be stored and collected about us, as well as the amount of time it can be held, can we protect ourselves against the kinds of data leaks that result, at best, in public humiliation, and at worst, in devastating identity theft.

Unfortunately, past legislation has done little to curb illegal file-sharing of music and movies on the Internet. However, the media companies are starting to finally take legal action. In November 2006, Universal Music Group filed a copyright-infringement suit against MySpace for allowing users to post and swap pirated versions of its musicians' videos and music. Universal is seeking damages of $150,000 per infraction—no small potatoes considering that a significant percentage of the site's 140 million users are probably in violation. Meanwhile, in January 2007, News Corp.'s Twentieth-Century Fox television studio subpoenaed YouTube to reveal the user who illegally uploaded digital copies of *The Simpsons* and *24*.[7] And, in February 2007, media conglomerate Viacom—which owns MTV, Nickelodeon, Black Entertainment Television (BET), and the Comedy Channel— formally requested that YouTube take down 100,000 clips, which, Viacom copyright lawyers assert, have been illegally posted on the video site. And in March 2007, Viacom pursued legal actions, suing the Google-owned company.

This sends a powerful message about the high price of intellectual property theft. And in October 2005, a coalition of publishers—Simon & Schuster, McGraw-Hill, John Wiley & Sons, and Penguin Group (USA)— sued Google for its plans to scan and digitize millions of copyrighted books. The more that companies follow this example in protecting the rights of their authors and artists, the more effective they will be in deterring digital piracy and reversing the cut-and-paste culture of the Web.

I would argue that regulation is most urgently needed in protecting our children against sexual predators and pornography on social-networking sites like MySpace. Bills have been proposed in several states that would require the e-mail addresses and instant messaging screen names of convicted sex offenders be registered so that they can be cross-referenced with social-networking sites' user databases. Such a protection from registered sex offenders *nationwide* would be even more effective. And MySpace, too, as the leading social-networking site, is creating a database with names and physical descriptions of sex offenders and developing technologies that could find and expel users with matching descriptions or profiles. But this only addresses part of the problem. What concerns me are all the offenders out there who are undetected because they have never been convicted, or those who join MySpace under false identities.

This is why government intervention can only go so far. The responsibility to protect young users really falls upon MySpace and similar sites to monitor content more vigilantly, and better police their sites to shield minors from indecent material or inappropriate sexual advances. Parents, too, can play a key role, using word filters to prevent minors from sending or receiving explicit messages. I would suggest that all photos sent to and by minors be screened for sexual content. Sites like MySpace should prohibit minors from including information in their profile that would identify them—such as a cell phone number or home address—and parents (and schools) should strongly discourage their children and teens from posting other potentially revealing information as well. The sites should implement more-secure background checks to ensure that when users set up their profiles, they can't lie about their age. And of course, when offenders are caught, they should be immediately and permanently banned from the site and, if appropriate, prosecuted.

And as a parent, I feel we need to enforce the laws designed to protect our kids from morally corrosive Internet content. I would urge enforcement of the 1998 Child Online Protection Act (COPA), the bipartisan legislation designed to protect children from online material deemed "indecent" as determined by "contemporary community standards." The law requires that operators of pornographic Web sites demand proof of age from their users before allowing them to access their content. COPA punishes Web-site operators with a $50,000 fine and a six-month prison term if they fail to comply with the law. Yet, despite its noble intention of criminalizing online pornographers who allow children to access their obscene material, COPA remains widely unenforced, as ACLU lawyers have taken advantage of the vague wording and successfully argued that it is impossible to define indecency "by an objective contemporary community standard." If the law does prove unenforceable in the courts, I would urge legislators to revise the law in such a way that the courts will accept it.

In May 2006, Congress passed the Deleting Online Predators Act, requiring that elementary and secondary schools ban access to social-networking sites on all school and library computers. The average schoolday is about seven hours long, and with computers now in every classroom, and student-to-teacher ratios often as high as 30 to 1, educators simply can't monitor what the kids are looking at all the time. By blocking access to social-networking sites, as well as to chat rooms and any other sites where minors may have access to sexual material or be "subject to" sexual advances in the schools, this bill, if signed, would go a long way to ensuring that our children are protected from harmful content, at least while on school grounds.

Is this censorship? If so, tell that to the parents of the ten-year-old girl who stumbled onto a hard-core anime porn Web site while doing research for her science project in the school library. Or to the parents of the curious twelve-year-old boy who accessed a site about bestiality and incest in the computer lab and showed it to his classmates.

Bringing It All Home

Which brings me to my final point: Parents must man the front lines in the battle to protect children from the evils lurking on the Web 2.0. In today's Web 2.0 world, one thing is clear—kids are spending more and more time online. And while this may be unavoidable, if you're a parent, when, where, and how your kid spends his or her time online is largely up to you. Move their computer to a family room, rather than allowing them to go online in the privacy of their bedrooms. This will help you to monitor the amount of time spent at MySpace and other sites that can monopolize their time at the expense of homework, exercise, or interacting with friends in the real world.

We can control when our kids are allowed online, where we keep the family computer, and especially now, with all the various Internet safety products available, what sites they visit and what content they see. With products like Net Nanny, Cybersitter, and SmartAlex, for example, parents can program their child's Internet browser to block specific sites or images, restrict chat and instant messaging to a "safe list" of friends, limit time online, control downloads, and block private information like phone numbers and addresses from leaving the computer. And by downloading the free parental notification software that MySpace unveiled in January 2007, parents can track the name, age, and location their children use to identify themselves on their MySpace page.

"But I don't want to spy on my kids," some parents might object. Well, neither do I. But I also don't let them watch the Playboy Channel, get in a car with strange men, or hop on a plane to Las Vegas for the weekend.

Parents have a responsibility to educate their kids about the dangers on the Internet. Just as we teach our kids to look both ways before they cross the street and not to take candy from strangers, so we must teach them safe online behaviors. And more important, we must be unwavering in our efforts to instill in them good judgment so that, if put in a compromising situation online, they will make the right—and safe—decision.

The Last Word

At the 2005 TED Conference, Kevin Kelly told the Silicon Valley crowd that we have a moral obligation to develop technology. "Imagine Mozart before the technology of the piano," he said. "Imagine Van Gogh before the technology of affordable oil paints. Imagine Hitchcock before the technology of film."

But technology doesn't create human genius. It merely provides new tools for self-expression. And if the democratized chaos of user-generated Web 2.0 content ends up replacing mainstream media, then there may not be a way for the Mozarts, Van Goghs, and Hitchcocks of the future to effectively distribute or sell their creative work.

Instead of developing technology, I believe that our real moral responsibility is to protect mainstream media against the cult of the amateur. We need to reform rather than revolutionize an information and entertainment economy that, over the last two hundred years, has reinforced American values and made our culture the envy of the world. Once dismantled, I fear that this professional media—with its rich ecosystem of writers, editors, agents, talent scouts, journalists, publishers, musicians, reporters, and actors—can never again be put back together. We destroy it at our peril.

So let's not go down in history as that infamous generation who, intoxicated by the ideal of democratization, killed professional mainstream media. Let's not be remembered for replacing movies, music, and books with YOU! Instead, let's use technology in a way that encourages innovation, open communication, and progress, while simultaneously preserving professional standards of truth, decency, and creativity. That's our moral obligation. It's our debt to both the past and the future.

notes

introduction

1. For more about Huxley's theory, see Jorge Luis Borges' 1939 essay "The Total Library."

2. Evan Hessel, "Shillipedia," *Forbes,* June 19, 2006.

3. http://mashable.com/2006/07/22/youtube-is-worlds-fastest-growing-website/

4. Scott Wooley, "Video Fixation," *Forbes,* October 16, 2006.

5. Audit Bureau of Circulations, September 2005, reports. BBC News, January 23, 2006. (http://news.bbc.co.uk/2/hi/entertainment/4639066.stm.)

6. Jeff Howe, "No Suit Required," *Wired,* September 2006.

7. Frank Ahrens, "Disney to Reorganize Its Lagging Movie Studios," *Washington Post,* July 20, 2006.

8. The term "cult of the amateur" was first coined by Nicholas Carr in his essay "The Amorality of Web 2.0," roughtype.com, October 3, 2005.

1 the great seduction

1. "Liquid Truth: Advice from the Spinmeisters," *PR Watch,* Fourth Quarter 2000, Volume 7, No. 4.

2. Antonio Regalado and Dionne Searcey, "Where Did That Video Spoofing Al Gore's Film Come From?" *Wall Street Journal,* August 3, 2006.

3. Michael Barbaro, "Wal-Mart enlists bloggers in PR campaign," *New York Times,* March 7, 2006.

4. "Ken Lay's Death Prompts Confusion on Wikipedia," *USA Today,* via Reuters, July 5, 2006.

5. Marshall Poe, "The Hive," *The Atlantic,* September 2006.

6. Kevin Kelly, "Scan This Book!" *New York Times Magazine,* May 14, 2006.

7. www.AMillionPenguins.com.

8. Reuters, "Publisher launches its first 'wiki' novel," February 1, 2007.

9. Chris Anderson, *The Long Tail,* Hyperion, 2006.

10. Trevor Butterworth, "Time for the Last Post," *Financial Times,* February 17, 2006.

11. http://blog.guykawasaki.com/2007/01/a_review_of_my_.html.

12. Brookes Barnes, "Big TV's Broadband Blitz," *Wall Street Journal,* August 1, 2006.

2 the noble amateur

1. Interview with author, August 24, 2006.

2. Stacy Schiff, "Know It All: Can Wikipedia Conquer Expertise?" *The New Yorker,* July 31, 2006.

3. Ibid.

4. Marshall Poe, "The Hive," *The Atlantic,* September 2006.

5. CNET News, March 13, 2001, and January 2, 2002.

6. Nicholas Lemann, "Amateur Hour: Journalism Without Journalists," *The New Yorker,* August 7 & 14, 2006.

7. Ibid.

8. Matt Drudge to National Press Club, June 2, 1998.

9. Interview with author.

10. Interview with author, March 17, 2006.

11. Nicholas Lemann, "Amateur Hour: Journalism Without Journalists," *The New Yorker*, August 7 & 14, 2006.

12. Ibid.

13. Robert J. Samuelson, "A Web of Exhibitionists," *Washington Post*, September 20, 2006.

14. Jürgen Habermas, Acceptance speech for the Bruno Kreisky Prize for the Advancement of Human Rights, March 9, 2006.

15. William Grimes, "You're a Slow Reader? Congratulations," *New York Times*, September 22, 2006.

16. Kevin Kelly, "Scan This Book!" *New York Times Magazine*, May 14, 2006.

17. Ibid.

18. Eric Stuer, "The Infinite Album," *Wired*, September 14, 2006.

19. Open Debate, "Can Anyone Be a Designer?" *Fast Company*, October 2006.

20. Louise Story, "Super Bowl Glory for Amateurs with Video Cameras," *New York Times*, September 27, 2006.

21. Glenn Reynolds, *Army of Davids*, Nelson, 2006.

3 truth and lies

1. Nancy Jo Sales, "Click Here for Conspiracy," *Vanity Fair*, September 2006.

2. John Markoff, "Attack of the Zombie Computers Is Growing Threat," *New York Times*, January 7, 2007.

3. Joanne Green, "Blind Date," *Miami New Times*, September 14, 2006.

4. Laura Parker, "Courts Are Asked to Crack Down on Bloggers, Web Sites," *USA Today*, October 2, 2006.

5. Ibid.

6. Amy Tan, "Personal Errata," from *The Opposite of Fate*, Penguin Putnam, 2003.

7. "Sock Puppet Bites Man," *New York Times* editorial, September 13, 2006.

8. Jon Fine, "The Strange Case of LonelyGirl15," *BusinessWeek*, September 11, 2006.

9. Howard Kurtz, "Loneliness, Lies, and Videotape," *Washington Post*, September 18, 2006.

10. Tom Glocer, transcript of speech given at the Globes Media Conference in Tel Aviv on Monday, December 11, 2006. http://tomglocer.com/blogs/sample_weblog/archive/2006/12/12/142.aspx

11. Sara Kehaulani Goo, "Videos on Web Widen Lens on Conflict," *Washington Post*, July 25, 2006.

12. Charles C. Mann, "Blogs+Spam=trouble," *Wired*, September 2006.

13. Brian Grow and Ben Elgin, with Moira Herbst, "Click Fraud," *BusinessWeek*, October 2, 2006.

14. Ibid.

15. Tom Zeller Jr., "Gaming the Search Engine, in a Political Season," *New York Times*, November 6, 2006.

16. Edelman PR Press Release, January 23, 2006.

17. Caroline McCarthy, "Paris Hilton Showcases YouTube's New Ad Concept," cnet.com (News), August 22, 2006.

18. Jamin Warren and John Jurgenson, "The Wizards of Buzz," *Wall Street Journal*, February 10, 2007.

19. Charles Mackay, *Extraordinary Popular Delusions*, Harriman House Classics, 2003.

4 the day the music died [side a]

1. Joel Selvin, "For S.F. rockers, Tower Records was where it was all happening—now the party's over," *San Francisco Chronicle*, October 19, 2006.

2. *The Financial Times*, October 12, 2006, based on research by International Federation of the Phonographic Industry (IFPI).

3. "Ann Powers Remembers Tower Records," *Los Angeles Times*, October 11, 2006.

4. Dave Kusek and Gerd Leonhard, *The Future of Music: Manifesto for the Digital Music Revolution*, Berklee Press, 2005.

5. Recording Industry Association of America.

6. Richard Waters, "MySpace seeks to become a force in online music sales," *The Financial Times*, September 1, 2006.

5 the day the music died [side b]

1. www.victorianweb.org/authors/dickens/pva/pva75.html

2. www.victorianweb.org/authors/dickens/pva/pva76.html

3. Jay Epstein, "The World According to Edward," *Slate,* October 31, 2005.

4. *Hollywood Reporter,* December 21, 2006.

5. Sharon Waxman, "After Hype Online, 'Snakes on a Plane' Is Letdown at Box Office," *New York Times,* August 21, 2006.

6. Frank Ahrens, "Disney to Reorganize Its Lagging Movie Studios," *Washington Post,* July 20, 2006.

7. Yuanzhe Cai and Kurt Scherf, "Internet Video: Direct to Consumer Services," Park Associates Report, November 2006.

8. Mark Porter, "Competition Is Killing Independent U.S. Bookstores," Reuters, December 26, 2006.

9. David Streitfield, "Bookshops' latest and sad plot twist," *Los Angeles Times,* February 7, 2006.

10. *San Antonio Business Journal,* November 24, 2006.

11. Katharine Q. Seelye, "In Tough Times, a Redesigned Journal," the *New York Times,* December 4, 2006.

12. Katharine Q. Seelye, "Newspaper Circulation Falls Sharply," *New York Times,* October 31, 2006.

13. Ibid.

14. Michael Wolff, "Panic on 43rd Street," *Vanity Fair,* September 2006.

15. "Ad woes worsen at Big Newspapers," *Wall Street Journal,* October 20, 2006.

16. Maria Aspan, "Great for Craigslist But Not for Newspapers," *New York Times,* November 28, 2006.

17. "Who Killed the Newspaper?" *The Economist,* August 24, 2006.

18. Katharine Q. Seelye, "Times Company Announces 500 Job Cuts," *New York Times,* September 21, 2005.

19. Katharine Q. Seelye, "Los Angeles Times Publisher Is Ousted," *New York Times,* October 6, 2006. Katharine Q. Seelye, "Los Angeles Paper Ousts Top Editor," *New York Times,* November 8, 2006.

20. David Carr, "Gruner and Jahr Chief Intends to Cut Costs by $25 Million," *New York Times,* August 7, 2004.

21. Philip Weiss, "A Guy Named Craig," *New York* magazine, January 16, 2006.

22. Michael Wolff, "Panic on 43rd Street," *Vanity Fair*, September 2006.

23. Katharine Q. Seelye, "A Newspaper Investigates Its Future," *New York Times*, October 12, 2006.

24. Who Killed the Newspaper?" *The Economist*, August 24, 2006.

25. Michael Wolff, "Panic on 43rd Street," *Vanity Fair*, September 2006.

26. "Who Killed the Newspaper?" *The Economist*, August 24, 2006.

27. eMarketer Report, October 17, 2006.

28. Tim Weber, "YouTubers To Get Ad Money Share," BBC News, January 27, 2007.

6 moral disorder

1. Suzanne Sataline, "That Sermon You Heard on Sunday May Be from the Web," *Wall Street Journal*, November 13, 2006.

2. Karoun Demirjian, "Denise Pope Comments on Student Plagiarism," *Christian Science Monitor*, May 11, 2006.

3. Matt Assad, "How Online Gambling Toppled Greg Hogan's World," *Morning Call*, August 17, 2006.

4. George T. Ladd and Nancy M. Petry, "Disordered Gambling Among University-Based Medical and Dental Patients: A Focus on Internet Gambling," *Psychology of Addictive Behaviors*, March 2002, Vol. 16, No. 1, 76–79.

5. Mattathias Schwartz, "The Hold-'Em Hold Up," *New York Times Magazine*, June 11, 2006.

6. Robyn Greenspan, "Porn Pages Reach 260 Million," Internetnews.com, September 5, 2003.

7. *Pediatrics: the Official Journal of the American Academy of Pediatrics*, Vol. 19, No. 2, February 2007, pp. 247–57.

8. Nerve.com, "The Prurient Interest: An Eighth Grader Weighs In," October 10, 2006.

9. Joe Garofoli, "Families of sexually abused girls sue MySpace," alleging negligence," *The San Francisco Chronicle*, January 19, 2007.

10. January W. Payne, "Caught in the Web," *Washington Post,* November 14, 2006.

11. "My Virtual Life," *BusinessWeek,* May 1, 2006.

12. Laura Conaway, "Rape Still Haunting Cyberspace," *Village Voice* online, December 15, 2006.

7 **1984 (version 2.0)**

1. Daniel Lee, "Lost and Found: Info on 260,000 Patients," *Indiana Star,* October 25, 2006.

2. Katie Weeks, "Fast-Growing Medical Identity Theft Has Lethal Consequences," *San Diego Business Journal,* October 16, 2006.

3. Tom Zeller Jr., "For Victims, Repairing ID Theft Can Be Grueling," *New York Times,* October 1, 2005.

4. Clive Thompson, "Open-Source Spying," *New York Times Magazine,* December 3, 2006.

5. Alexi Mostrous and Rob Evans, "Google Will Be Able to Keep Tabs on All of Us," *The Guardian,* November 3, 2006.

6. Richard Wray, "Google Users Promise Artificial Intelligence," *The Guardian,* May 23, 2006.

8 **solutions**

1. James Rainey, "Editor James O'Shea unveils Web initiative at Times," *Los Angeles Times,* January 24, 2007.

2. IFPI, Digital Music Report 2007.

3. Nielsen SoundScan report, December 14, 2006.

4. Steve Jobs, "Thoughts on music," www.apple.com, February 7, 2007.

5. Devin Leonard, "Rockin' Along in the Shadow of iTunes," *Fortune,* February 19, 2007.

6. Joshua Chaffin, "EMI Goes Radical on Digital Rights," Andrew Edgecliffe-Johnson and Richard Waters, *Financial Times,* February 12, 2007.

7. Nicole Urbanowicz, "Fox Subpoenas YouTube over Pirated TV Shows," *Wall Street Journal,* January 26, 2007.

acknowledgments

began with a confession, so let me end with one, too.

I confess that, as a writer, I remain a bit of an amateur. This is my first book, and I'm still learning the craft of this complex business. It has been my great fortune, however, to have received a first-rate literary education from a remarkable group of professional agents, editors, publishers, and marketers.

This education began in New York City one morning in late 2005. I was walking down Broadway toward Times Square. Tucked under my arm were the first 100 pages of a "book" that I'd been working on since FOO Camp 2004. Part anti-Web 2.0 polemic, part Silicon Valley dystopia, part paean to Alfred Hitchcock's movie *Vertigo*, part autobiography, this muddled first draft was classic amateur self-indulgence—100 percent unreadable and 100 percent unpublishable.

I found myself in Steve Hanselman's garret of an office on Forty-second Street, just off Broadway. Steve and his partner, Cathy Hemming—both ex–HarperCollins senior executives—had just opened a literary agency called LevelFive Media. With over twenty-five years of experience in the publishing business, Steve instinctively knew what I wanted to say better than I did.

"An anti-Web 2.0 polemic," Steve said. "That's what you are really trying to write."

Exactly. So, with Cathy's and Steve's expert guidance, and under the editorial tutelage of LevelFive's Julia Serebrinsky, I deleted those original 100 pages and started again. Cathy introduced me to Jonathan Last, the online editor of the *Weekly Standard* magazine. Jonathan graciously agreed to look at an article comparing Web 2.0 ideology to Marxism. That article, expertly edited by Jonathan, got published in February 2006 and became an instant hit, getting syndicated on CBS News and transforming me into the *bête noire* of the digital utopian crowd.

I remained an amateur. But now, at least, I was a controversial one.

When, in the spring of 2006, Steve sold my book to Roger Scholl's Currency imprint at Doubleday, I assumed that I'd made it into the exalted ranks of professional authors. How wrong I was. This is when my serious learning began.

"Any advice on how to write a first book?" I asked Roger when we first met.

"Just have fun," he replied.

I've had fun. But it's been the Puritan version—the sweaty fun of learning a craft, the Sisyphean fun of turning myself into a professional writer. Working with Roger and ever-responsive assistant editor Talia Krohn has been an intensely educative six months. They taught me the importance of focus, economy, organization, sticking to the preexisting plan—above all, writing *one* book at a time. The most lucid bits of *The Cult of the Amateur* were squeezed out of me and then polished up by Roger and Talia. Please blame me for any amateurish digressions that even their eagle editorial eyes missed.

There would be no *Cult of the Amateur* without Steve, Roger, Talia, Cathy, Jonathan, or Julia. As agents, publishers, and editors, each represents a paragon of the mainstream media ecosystem. I'm just the symbolic tip of a very large iceberg—what in Silicon Valley we call the "front end" of a business enterprise.

Nor would there be a book without the noble efforts of the marketing and sales team at Doubleday. The only bigger fallacy than anyone being able to write a book is that anyone can market and sell one. Web 2.0 book publishing start-ups like Lulu and iUniverse seduce amateur writers with the false promise of instant mass distribution. But, as even Chris Anderson reminds us, the vast majority of books sell fewer than 100 copies. What distinguishes a mainstream publisher like Doubleday are the incredibly rich sales and marketing resources that they offer their writers. I've been particularly lucky to work with Doubleday's deputy publisher, Michael Palgon, as well as David Drake and Liz Hazelton in publicity, and Meredith McGinnis in marketing, Rebecca Gardener in foreign rights, and Louis Quayle in domestic rights. I would also like to thank my own small but highly professional marketing, research, and technology team of Catrin Betts, Sabine Elser, and Peter Rowland, who have contributed significantly to this project, from before the beginning till after the end. Finally, I would like to thank Nicholas Carr, whose richly insightful "The Amorality of Web 2.0" essay (2005) about the cult of the amateur helped define and refine my own arguments in this book.

Thanks to all of you for an unforgettable education. I only hope that this little book does some justice to your splendid job of finding, polishing, and selling talent.

—Berkeley, December 27, 2006

index

index